TODAY IS THE DAY.

LIVE IT!

Edge of Comfort to Center of Impact

Featuring Changemaker Voices from
California to Uganda

Authored and Compiled by

JODI HOPE GRINWALD CPC, ELI-MP.

Edited by Heather McCulloch

TODAY IS THE DAY.
LIVE IT!

TODAY is the DAY
PUBLISHING

www.TodayIsTheDayLiveIt.com

TABLE OF CONTENTS

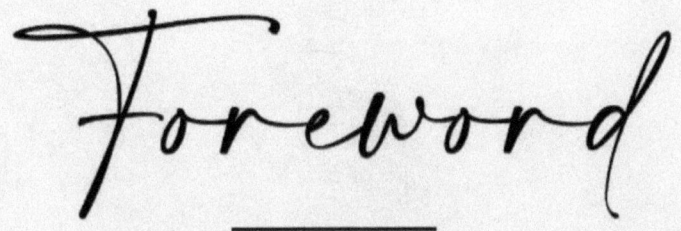

Foreword

CHANGEMAKER: FRED C. WASIAK

To my family — Your quiet courage, kindness, and love inspire me every day to believe that small acts create big change.

"True changemaking isn't about titles, credentials,
or grand gestures—it's about purpose, connection, and
the consistent, heartfelt actions of everyday people."

– FRED C. WASIAK

ometimes, opportunities don't knock—they whisper. They show up in the form of a last-minute email, a spontaneous meeting, or a short twelve-minute window of time. That's how I met Jodi. She was seeking out the Food Bank of South Jersey to join the New Jersey Business & Industry Association (NJBIA) and requested my help in leading the Southern Region for its statewide Nonprofit Council. I wasn't originally part of the plan, but Jodi's instinct to reach out set everything in motion.

We had never worked together before, but we shared something foundational: both of us had spent meaningful time serving in the YMCA movement. Although our paths never crossed, we immediately recognized a shared commitment to purpose and people.

At the first statewide Nonprofit Council kickoff, Jodi gave me twelve minutes (I thought she must be joking) to open the seminar. Just twelve minutes to build energy, spark trust, and set the tone for over seventy-five nonprofit leaders. And somehow, it worked. In that short window, barriers dropped.

People leaned in. A sense of belonging began to take root. I could've used thirty, but Jodi—ever the strategist—understands the power of clarity and pace. She moves with intention and always keeps the greater vision in mind. I still joke with her about it today!

As we continued to connect through mentoring conversations and shared think tanks, I watched the evolution of Today is the Day Changemakers. What began as a podcast became a platform. Then, a movement. And eventually, a community.

Together, we arrived at a simple truth: authentic changemakers don't need fancy titles, impressive resumes, or the loudest voice in the room. What they need is a sense of purpose. A calling to serve, to lead, and to make things better—not for applause, but because they care.

Whether in nonprofit missions or purpose-centered businesses, it's the humble, consistent, heartfelt actions that leave the deepest mark. True changemaking is grounded in connection, not credentials.

One of the myths we fall for is that making a difference requires something big—a campaign, a platform, a revolution. But what we've discovered through the Changemakers community is that it's often the smallest moments that matter most. A kind word. A thoughtful gesture. A challenge met with courage. These quiet acts ripple outward, inspiring others to do the same.

Each guest on the Today is the Day Changemakers podcast has added to that ripple. Their stories—real, raw, and inspiring—have created a living archive of what it means to lead with intention. One guest reflected on the choice to act with kindness rather than convenience, a small decision that shaped someone's life trajectory. Another spoke about navigating failure and finding clarity not in success, but in trying again.

That ripple didn't stop with the podcast. It expanded across continents. What began as local conversations turned into two International Changemakers Virtual Forums, bringing together leaders from around the world. These weren't influencers chasing platforms. They were individuals connected by shared values—like-hearted people with a collective purpose. They came together because of Jodi. They stayed because of the community she cultivated: one rooted in inclusion, understanding, and the powerful energy of the collective.

What makes all this possible is Jodi's unwavering belief in building tables—not just waiting for a seat at one. Her story is rooted in resilience. Growing up in Brooklyn, surviving trauma, and navigating life with undiagnosed learning differences, she didn't take the traditional path. She forged her own—becoming a nonprofit leader, a certified coach, a CEO, and most of all, a builder. When doors didn't open, she made new ones. And she held them open for others.

From launching the Zzak G. Applaud Our Kids Foundation to founding The Connective, she continues to build spaces where voices are heard—not filtered. Where people rise together—not alone. The Connective is more than a network. It's a global alliance of purpose-driven professionals who align, collaborate, and grow—with no permission needed.

And I'm equally honored to serve alongside colleagues at the Food Bank of South Jersey—individuals who show up each day with courage, heart, and quiet resilience. In their own powerful way, they offer hope where it's needed most. They are everyday changemakers, too.

This book—*Live It*—is an extension of that vision. It brings together the unified voice of individuals who have chosen to show up, again and again, with heart and hope. You'll read stories of courage, trial and error, resilience, and quiet determination. You'll meet people who said "yes" to something greater than themselves—and in doing so, helped others rise.

But most of all, this book is an invitation. A reminder that changemaking doesn't belong to a chosen few. It lives in all of us. It lives in the teacher who stays late to encourage a student. In the entrepreneur who builds a business around purpose. In the neighbor who listens. In you. You won't find perfection in these pages—but you'll find purpose. You'll find real people doing real work with extraordinary heart.

So, take these stories in. Let them stir something in you. Let them remind you that you don't need permission, a title, or a spotlight to make a difference. Just a willingness to care, and the courage to act.

Because the world doesn't just need more leaders. It needs you—just as you are. Thank you, Jodi.

LIVE IT!

Embrace the *moment*

We are all everyday changemakers – each of us contains the ability to make an impact in our own way.

What inspired Fred to be a changemaker?

AUTHOR'S REPLY:

I'm inspired to be a changemaker because I believe transformation begins with mastering self and growing as whole persons, in spirit, mind, body, and heart. When individuals and organizations live this truth, they create communities grounded in purpose and connection— sparking change that extends far beyond themselves.

NOW IT IS YOUR TURN...

What inspires you to be a changemaker?

Fred invites you to reflect with two additional questions:

What is one thing you need to do to move your vision forward?

When was the last time you took a walk in nature?

Visit the "Meet the Changemakers" section at the back of the book to connect with and learn more about all of the authors featured in **LIVE IT!**

Introduction

One Decision. Extraordinary Impact.

~ Jodi Hope Grinwald

There are people who grow up believing that they can do anything. I wasn't one of them.

I dealt with what a lot of people deal with - impostor syndrome. The "I'm not good enough," "I'm not smart enough," "I'm not pretty enough"—these are the songs that so many of us sing. Sometimes they are loud, blaring in our minds; other times they are a soft whisper, feeding our fears.

In time, with every small step and each unexpected win, my belief in myself slowly grew. Life handed me twists and turns I never saw coming, and somehow each one pushed me in ways I never knew I needed.

When I finally allowed myself to gravitate toward the work that mattered most to me, something unexpected happened. I began to meet extraordinary people.

One decision led to another, and soon I was working with, speaking with, and learning from changemakers across industries, backgrounds, and countries.

I will never forget the moment someone unexpectedly said to me, "You're the changemaker." It was then that I realized how the outside world sees me differently from how I see myself.

My hope for you is that you realize you, too, are a changemaker.

This Book is For You

For the person sitting at a desk, feeling invisible, wondering if anyone truly sees them.

For the leader who carries the weight of every decision, shouldering responsibility even when their own strength is being tested.

For the entrepreneur standing alone in the unknown, building something from nothing, while no one sees the quiet courage it takes.

For the dreamer who wonders if they're ever enough, measuring their worth against a world that rarely slows down to notice.

For the person driving to work every day, feeling like there has to be more than just this.

For the one who aches for connection but has no idea where to find the kind that feels real.

This is for you, every version of you.
The seen and unseen.
The steady and the breaking open.

You are not behind.
Your voice matters more than you can even imagine.

The Heart Behind These Pages

As you read these words on the page, on a screen, or one day listen in audio form, there's something I want you to know.

This moment feels like a miracle.

For some, publishing a book might seem simple. For me, having these voices gathered here and acknowledging the remarkable journey that brought us together feels nothing short of extraordinary.

What follows is a mosaic of lives that may never have crossed paths if not for the platform I built for one purpose: to open space for all to be heard and valued.

Thirty-one voices across sectors and stages of life; leaders, builders, creatives, nonprofit professionals, and everyday changemakers have come together to share pieces of their lives with honesty and courage. In the pages ahead, you will find testaments of resilience, roadmaps to transformation, and reminders that no title, follower count, or bank balance defines the value of a voice.

At the end of every chapter, you'll find an Embrace the Moment section: two questions the author asks you directly, inviting you to open your mind and walk closer to the edge of your comfort zone.

Themes That Travel Well

As you move through the following chapters, you'll notice themes that apply to you no matter your title, industry, or zip code:

Resilience In Motion

A muscle you build—one decision, one challenge, one small act at a time.

Redefining Direction

Feeling lost isn't failure; it's the starting line for reinvention, clarity, and purpose.

Leadership Without the Pedestal

Influence redefined as collaboration, empathy, and the choice to use your voice so others can find theirs.

The Power of Giving

Not just in dollars, but in time, attention, creativity, and open doors—acts that multiply impact.

Community As Strength

The right people don't just ride along; they help hold the map, adjust the sails, and remind you when you're drifting.

Practical Sparks

Not theory, but real-life experiences you can use right now in your work, relationships, and life.

Read these as inspiration, not instructions.

How to Use These Pages

Find the way that works best for you.

Read straight through or jump to the chapter that is calling you.

Use the prompts in a journal, on a walk, or in conversation with a friend or colleague.

If you're leading a team or organization, consider choosing one chapter each week and working through the prompts together—opening space for connection, perspective, and meaningful dialogue.

You Are Invited

I invite you to tune out the distractions, settle in, and let the courageous voice within you speak. Let each chapter encourage you, challenge you, and remind you that momentum beats perfection.

When you are willing to stand at the edge of your comfort zone, that is where you will discover your true center of impact.

This is your invitation to believe in the power of one voice: your own.

CHAPTER 1

When Your Why is Greater Than Your How:
The Power of the

First Step

CHANGEMAKER: JODI HOPE GRINWALD, CPC, ELI-MP

To my daughters, Gabriella and Sienna—two beautiful humans who have grown into extraordinary women. You are so special and bring light to all that you do. I am endlessly proud of you both. Always remember: MGC.

"Today is the day! You cannot go back to yesterday,
and you do not yet own tomorrow."

– JODI HOPE GRINWALD, CPC, ELI-MP

The Firsts That Shape Us

The first job.

The first risk.

The first time someone says yes when you aren't even sure you deserve it.

These moments shape us, even when we don't recognize them as beginnings. They become turning points whose meaning only reveals itself in hindsight.

This book exists because of a series of firsts in my life, moments when I stepped into something without knowing how it would work, only that my why was bigger than my fear. It also exists because of the people who crossed my path at pivotal moments that at the time seemed ordinary. The unexpected meetings that changed my direction. The conversations that seemed small but carried weight that I couldn't understand until later.

Not all firsts come with someone holding your hand. Some come from exhaustion, some from hope. Some because staying where you are hurts more than stretching into something unknown. Most come from a quiet inner voice that whispers, try anyway.

And firsts don't stop. They don't end at a certain age. They continue throughout our lives in different rooms, with different people, in moments we rarely recognize as transformative until much later.

Without the puzzle pieces you're about to read, without the people who showed up at just the right time, without the decisions I made while overthinking and second-guessing myself, nothing else in this book, including the thirty other voices you'll meet, would exist.

As you read, I hope you think about the decisions you're making right now. The ones that keep you up at night replaying scenarios. The ones that feel like they only impact you, but in truth ripple out to the people you love, the people you haven't met yet, and even the people you may never meet.

Sometimes the smallest decisions, especially the ones born out of exhaustion, hope, or blind faith, become the steps that change everything.

When the World Felt Too Loud

I grew up quiet, shy, and trying not to be seen because being seen often meant being hurt.

My parents separated when I was in sixth grade. That was a pivotal moment in my childhood, especially because I did not know one person in my class at that time who was in the same situation. It felt isolating.

Only weeks before starting ninth grade, I was assaulted by a girl on my block to the point that I had to be homeschooled my entire freshman year. With in-home traction and a ripped cartilage in front of my heart, numbness in my left arm, my life felt shattered. As everyone excitedly entered high school, I was scared to leave my home. As a young teenager going through extreme trauma, I didn't understand then how deeply those moments would shape so many things in my future.

I became afraid of anything that carried risk, physical, emotional, or public. I wanted to stay small, protected, unnoticed. I feared judgment and exposure.

I changed high schools three times. The girl who assaulted me was going to the same school I was zoned for, so in sophomore year, I went to a different school, taking two buses and walking four blocks. During the first snowfall that year, I fell and broke my elbow running for the bus. It was enough for me and time to move. My mother, sister, and I decided to start over somewhere new. So, from Brooklyn we went to Staten Island. I spent the remainder of high school making just a few friends. I continued to be the quiet and shy student, striving to get through those last two years as quickly as possible.

The Industries That Taught Me Connection

Looking back, if I had a teacher or a therapist who could have helped me during that traumatic time, maybe I would have felt more supported when I needed it most. Those were the two professions calling me. But I quickly found out that I enjoyed working more than I did sitting in the classroom, so although I went to college for a short time, I decided to work full-time.

My dad and I got really close at the end of high school and the beginning of college. He became my best friend, coach, mentor, and ultimately my business coach. I am grateful for all the time he gave me whenever I had anything to celebrate or any challenges.

He helped me get my first real job in NYC, where I worked for his friend as a manufacturer's representative. His friend mentored me in that role. Imagine me, the quiet and shy person, cold-calling buyers of major retail stores. I scheduled them to come to our showroom on 34th Street and 5th Avenue to do presentations of our products. At first, I was petrified, and I was lucky to learn from someone who saw something in me. Slowly, I was awakening. I just didn't know it at the time.

Although I loved that job, I stopped loving the commute, so I entered industries that had nothing to do with one another. I took jobs that were right in front of me—from a manufacturer's representative for women's accessories and children's toys to a computer consulting firm, to working for a national demolition contractor.

Each role taught me something essential: all industries are built on connection. Those jobs weren't random. All were getting me ready to meet a part of myself I hadn't yet met.

The Door That Opened Anyway

In 2005, I was unemployed with two daughters, Gabriella, seven, and Sienna, four. I pounded the pavement, responding to companies using Monster.com. At that point, I was thirty-four years old and tired of finding just jobs. I wanted to find a career path. However, with no degree, I carried the weight of impostor syndrome and was judged by others because I couldn't check the bachelor's degree box.

I was grateful for all I learned up until then, but it was time to find direction. After applying for several jobs that day, I went back into the system later in the evening. I found a role that sounded perfect for me, but there was one problem: I didn't have all they asked for—you guessed it, a bachelor's degree. It was for a regional director at a nonprofit. I uploaded my resume and cover letter, hit apply, and never expected to hear back. Yet in the back of my mind, I thought to myself how incredible it would be if I could get this position.

Days passed, and I forgot about it. Then the phone rang. It was someone from the American Heart Association. They wanted to do a phone interview. That led to an in-person interview, and then a panel interview that lasted three hours.

I remember I was driving when my cell phone rang a month later. I pulled over to hear, "We would like to offer you the job." I really thought they forgot all about me. When I went in for each interview, I visualized myself showing up for work each day in that office. As I waited to be called back, I thought about how it would feel to drive there daily.

I have always believed in the power of visualization. It isn't just wishful thinking; it is aligning your energy with possibility. It is more than mindset; it is trust in something greater than circumstance. Visualization has worked for me many times in my life, and I hold it as one of the most powerful tools we can use to create what we want.

I didn't realize that this yes from the American Heart Association would change the course of my life, but it did.

When Mission Found Me

Nonprofit work was a different world. I wasn't selling a product. I was selling purpose.

I remember feeling overwhelmed at first by the daunting fundraising goals; yet I had always met or exceeded my goals at my other jobs. My dad told me to do what I naturally did: connect with people. Ask questions. Care. Be genuine. Get to know the people. When we are in scarcity mode, it makes things seem more impossible than possible. So, forget the goal exists and give 100 percent every day because you can't give more than that. Once you give 100 percent, it doesn't matter what the goal is anymore.

Connection became my compass. I created the mantra that I later taught my team: lead with mission, and the money will follow.

The Power of Being Seen

My first Heart Walk chair was Anthony Hooper, then senior vice president of global commercial operations and president, Americas, Japan, and Intercontinental Regions for Bristol-Myers Squibb (BMS).

At my first event, just weeks after I started at the American Heart Association, I had to introduce myself as the new regional director and Tony as the new chair to those attending the Heart Walk celebration. Remember, I was quiet, shy, and public speaking was not something I had ever longed for in my life. I was great one-on-one, but in a room of over 100 people, I was terrified. In that moment, I thought, why did I say yes to this job and do this to myself?

He noticed and said, "What can they take away from you that you came into this room with?"

Nothing. They can take nothing.

That moment, when put into perspective, gave me a little more courage and confidence. It wasn't that they could take anything away from me. It was judgment that I feared. But Tony again assured me that it is not for me to worry about. It is hard to let people think what they will, but it is true that they cannot take anything physically away from you that will change you.

I remember thinking, here I am among leaders and people with major degrees, high-level executives, and I am leading this event with them, steering the traffic, creating something from nothing, inviting them to serve on my Executive Leadership Team. It was a full-circle moment that reminded me how far I had come from the girl who once feared her own voice.

Tony wasn't just the chair of my Heart Walk, but also a mentor. When my father later became ill, he even tried to help me find clinical trials. His ongoing kindness helped me tremendously throughout my first year in the nonprofit, and he was a true example of what a leader should be. While at BMS, he was beloved by his employees. I feel grateful to have met and worked with him.

The Nonprofit Bootcamp

I moved up quickly. After eighteen months, I became senior regional director, supervising staff and working with executives from multiple counties to chair and lead our events. I was blessed to work with another incredible mentor from the American Heart Association, who was, back then, the head of Human Resources for our affiliate, Patti Witschger. She believed in me and mentored me as I moved up the ranks, and I will forever be grateful to her. She taught me the beautiful lesson about being a vault in business.

The American Heart Association became my nonprofit bootcamp. It was where I learned leadership, mission, communication, resilience, and how to stand in a room without shrinking. The old me with impostor syndrome and fears would still pop up every so often, and I would have to remind myself how far I had come.

After more than seven years and in the role of executive director, I felt a pull to grow. I decided it was time to leave and secured a position at another nonprofit organization with a larger title, team, territory, bigger salary, and, of course, more responsibility.

Michael Weamer, then executive vice president for the American Heart Association, called me. He wasn't the one who hired me, and I did not directly report to him, but he was the lead for our affiliate at the time. As we were talking, he said, "I hear you are leaving us."

He reminded me about the benchmark awards that I had received while working there and said amazing things about how much my work was valued. To my surprise, he offered me a one-time stay bonus. It was another surreal moment. I was one of the lowest-paid regional directors when I started there because I had no experience in the nonprofit sector; yet now I was being valued.

It took me a moment to answer him as I considered staying, knowing that I was taking on a much larger territory and responsibilities in my next role. In the end, I knew I had made my decision, and it was hard for me to turn down that offer. Still, I knew it was time for a new chapter.

I accepted a vice president of development role with another organization, managing teams across multiple states and overseeing a million-dollar goal. The role stretched me. It was exhilarating and uncomfortable all at once. I often asked myself if I had made the right decision to leave a place that felt familiar. But comfort, I have learned, can either bring peace or prevent growth.

It was exciting meeting so many new people in areas where I had no connections. I went from working in one state to five. It was meaningful, but burnout was creeping in.

The Burnout That Wouldn't Quiet Down

There were videos of my daughters saying, "Mom, watch me," while they tried to show me their cartwheels or splits they worked so hard to perfect. Yet there I was, typing away on the laptop, never looking up to really see what they were showing me. That laptop traveled everywhere with me: dance rehearsals, play rehearsals, everywhere. I was making a difference. I threw myself into my work. My children learned quickly about nonprofit work and got to experience wonderful things while learning what it means to give back.

Those sixty to eighty-hour workweeks took a toll on me. I loved the mission and the people, but I was losing myself and missing moments.

I share this message with all parents: shut the computer down, turn the ringer off, and watch the cartwheels, go to the games, and be there to experience as much as you can. They remember the moments you didn't show up, and even though they forgive you, they don't ever really forget them.

I had this calling inside at this point, but I didn't know what it was. It felt like something in me was shifting. I was exhausted, but I loved how I was able to help others, make a difference, raise awareness, and connect people. Still, I was starting to feel totally fulfilled. I wanted to help people in a different way, but had no idea exactly how.

I was feeling antsy to figure it out, but also very stuck, loving the salary I was making and feeling like I should be so grateful to be where I was, providing more for my girls than I ever had. Not to mention my gratitude for finding my voice, becoming more confident, gaining the courage to speak up at tables where my voice sometimes didn't feel heard, and making so many new connections. Many of my sponsors, volunteers, and teams became like a second family to me.

The Breakfast That Shifted Something

During my time at the second nonprofit, I launched a Women's Breakfast series to raise funds and connect business leaders with our mission. One year, I needed a keynote speaker and remembered a conversation I had with a woman whose daughter attended the same conservatory as mine.

My daughter, Sienna, had asked to attend a sleepover at her home. I didn't know her well, but I learned she had once been on *The Oprah Winfrey Show* and was an author. Sienna thought that should be enough to let her go to the sleepover with her friend. I mean, if Oprah vetted her, then this should be an easy yes. I let Sienna go after having a conversation with the mom.

So, when I needed a speaker, I reached out on a whim, and she agreed.

Days before the event, her mentor passed away, and she wasn't sure she could make it. On the morning of breakfast, I woke up to snow. I was sure no one would come.

But they did. And so did she.

As she spoke, the snow fell softly outside the window. Somehow, a ray of sunlight broke through the cloudy sky and caught her face as she moved across the stage. It was a surreal moment when I looked back because of what happened next. I watched as the audience was brought to laughter, then to tears, and these strangers at round tables all left feeling incredibly connected. I stood in the back of the room, completely still.

It was like watching purpose in motion.

In that moment, something deep inside me whispered and eventually screamed, "That is what I want to do."

That night, I started researching coaching certification schools. But when I saw the tuition, my heart sank. With two daughters heading toward college, it felt impossible. So, I tucked the dream away.

But I didn't forget it. It followed me through every long drive through all of New Jersey, Pennsylvania, Delaware, and Washington, DC. I researched motivational speakers and listened to voices like Jason Goldberg, Lisa Nichols, and Brené Brown. Their stories kept me believing, maybe someday.

I told my dad and anyone who would listen that I thought I had found something I would really love to do, but I had no idea how I would make it happen. So, it got tucked away in the back of my mind.

The Promise

Through all those years, my father was my greatest supporter. He was my sounding board and my anchor. We spoke daily, even late at night when I was driving home from long events.

In October 2014, everything changed. My dad was diagnosed with ALS. Watching his body weaken while his mind stayed sharp was devastating.

The time came for him to decide what he wanted to do as he was on life support. He couldn't move anything besides his eyes and his lips. He no longer had a voice, and as he put it, he was rusting from the inside out. His pain was excruciating. The day he decided he wanted to be taken off life support, he mouthed that he wanted to see us one by one, alone, giving each of us his final advice and love.

When it was my turn, he looked at me and mouthed, "Promise me you will do what you want to do and help people. Promise me you will go back to school and get your certification."

He was in the hospital for fifty-nine days, and I was there for about fifty-four of them. While being on life-saving machines, he watched me in his room, Skyping in his bathroom, making it look like an office, because I needed to hire people for my team. I positioned the computer on the sink with my chair against the wall as his machines beeped in the far distance. I worked throughout the time he was in the hospital. He saw me juggling holding his hand when he would be awake, to waking up to me being on my laptop working. He knew that I wanted more, and right before leaving this earth, he was thinking about what I would do next.

I couldn't say no. I had no idea where I was going to find the money or the time, but I made a promise.

The day he left this earth broke me, but it also did something else.

A Table, a Chair, and Legacy

My dad adored Starbucks. He would sit at a table by the window and write songs there. He connected with everyone who walked in. He was a coach long before I understood what coaching truly was.

When we told the baristas at the Starbucks near the funeral home where we were holding his memorial in Red Bank, NJ, about his passing, the staff cried. They donated the coffee. Not too long after, they were going to remodel that Starbucks, and I received a call from one of the employees, Danielle, the barista who knew him well. She told me that she was given permission to give us the table and chairs he sat at when he was there.

That table sits with us still.

Connection isn't just an idea. It is a lifeline.

That moment showed me what real legacy looks like. It is not in awards or titles, followers or subscribers; it is in the connections we leave behind.

He used to say he practiced the religion of kindness, and he lived it. Every person he met felt seen, heard, and valued. His faith wasn't confined to a place of worship; it was reflected in how he treated others, how he showed up, and how he listened.

Claiming Connection

Not long after my father passed, I kept my promise. I enrolled for a double certification, Certified Professional Coach and Energy Leadership Index Master Practitioner. I still didn't have the time or the money, but what I had was a promise. It wasn't one I made to myself, although I learned something important. We don't need to promise someone else to give ourselves permission to do something that we really want. We also don't have to wait for a tragedy to happen to give us the confidence to move forward.

What I thought would be a professional development decision became a personal transformation. It stripped away everything I thought I knew about success and forced me to face what I valued. That training wasn't just to help me effectively coach others and help them find the answers within themselves; it taught me a lot about myself and revisiting things I too needed to work through.

During the training, they recommend that you have a niche. I realized my calling was not about one specific niche. It was about connection itself. I wanted to help people connect and reconnect to their purpose, their teams, their businesses, their clients, their donors, meet and exceed their goals, and, more importantly, make sure to always stay connected to themselves.

I claimed it.
Connection coaching.

It didn't fit into a box, but it fit me.

The Birth of AOK

About a year later, my sister, Melissa, and I sat in my backyard, trying to figure out how to honor our father's legacy. He found out in his mid-thirties that he was an operatic tenor. When he was younger, he had wanted to take voice lessons, but he couldn't afford them. His biggest deathbed regret was not being able to stand on stage and connect with audiences more. He took lessons when he could as he got older, and he performed when the opportunities arose. It was what he did in his downtime when he wasn't working full-time in New York City. He never got to see his dream become a reality on an ongoing basis.

However, he did write an incredible song about a homeless man he never met. He saw that man being taken away because he had passed away from frostbite in NYC. He thought how could a person leave this earth, die alone, and have no one there to cry for him? He had the song produced and put it on YouTube at "Zzak G. Homeless."

Then we found a way to honor our dad as well. With my nonprofit experience and my sister's organizational strengths, we created the Zzak G. Applaud Our Kids (AOK) Foundation, funding performing arts lessons for children with financial barriers across New Jersey. The children are funded from the ages of seven to eighteen if they continue to meet the financial needs requirements, and they are placed in performing arts schools close to their home that are pre-approved by our organization. We want to give children who need this creative connection the opportunity to experience something that our dad wished existed.

Before we went to open the bank account, I called the bank to ask how much was needed to open the nonprofit business account. They said, "A hundred dollars." We hadn't touched our father's wallet since he passed a year and a half before that day. We remembered that we left that last hundred-dollar crisp bill in there, and we had decided not to touch it or use it until then.

He started the foundation for us without knowing it.

The foundation became our shared mission, helping children with all abilities find their voice through music, dance, acting, instrumental instruction, and vocal performance. I also watched my sister step into her own voice, conquering her fear of public speaking and growing into the confident leader she was meant to be.

I believe our dad is so proud of the children in our programming and that he is sitting in the front row watching all the children perform as he did for his grandkids when they performed, yelling, "Fantastic." Thank goodness for our mom doing the same and helping us through the loss of our dad, even though they weren't together when he passed.

The Turning Point

All these moments, the firsts, the no's, the leaps of faith, the heartbreaks, and the building something from nothing, were leading me somewhere.

I didn't realize it at the time, but they were shaping the foundation for everything that would come next: the coaching and consulting business, the podcast, the forum, the connective, the Today is the Day ecosystem, and the book you're reading now.

They were teaching me that connection isn't just a philosophy. It is a lifeline.

Eventually, I understood something.

It is not always about finding a seat at someone else's table. Sometimes it is about building your own, the kind where every voice is heard, every story matters, and connection sits at the head.

LIVE IT!

Embrace the *moment*

We are all everyday changemakers – each of us contains the ability to make an impact in our own way.

What inspires Jodi to be a changemaker?

AUTHOR'S REPLY:

What inspires me to be a changemaker is connection, real human connection. It's the belief that small actions, honest conversations, and moments of courage can reach far beyond what we see. I am driven by the desire to do something that makes my corner of the world and beyond a better place. We take up space while we are here, and with that comes an extraordinary opportunity and responsibility to make an incredible difference.

My inspiration comes from watching people rise after hardship, from witnessing kindness practiced without an audience, and from knowing that the most powerful impact often begins quietly with one decision to care. I am inspired by the people who believed in me before I believed in myself, by mentors like my father whose wisdom shaped my values, and by those who showed me that leadership doesn't come from titles or applause, it comes from compassion and consistency.

Every time I see a child discovering their voice through the arts, a leader finding new purpose, or someone realizing they don't need permission to take their next step, I'm reminded why I do this work. Being a changemaker isn't about changing the whole world at once. It's about changing moments, helping others see what's possible when they choose connection over comparison, courage over comfort, and purpose over perfection, and trusting that those moments will carry forward far beyond where we stand.

Now it is your turn...

What inspires you to be a changemaker?

Jodi invites you to reflect with two additional questions:

When the fear of the unknown is less than the pain of what you already know, you will take your first step toward a goal. What in your life does that bring up for you?

What step small or large will you take today to get yourself closer to a goal or goals that you have?

Visit the "Meet the Changemakers" section at the back of the book to connect with and learn more about all of the authors featured in **LIVE IT!**

CHAPTER 2

Power of
Connection

CHANGEMAKER: JODI HOPE GRINWALD

To the newest, beautiful light in our family—my first grandbaby: I cannot wait to watch you grow and see you smile as you discover the world in your own magical way. You fill our family with more love than words can hold.

"Collaboration starts when titles stop defining
us and connection starts aligning us."

– JODI HOPE GRINWALD

Throughout my career, people often talked about getting a seat at the table. But when I finally began earning those seats, I realized just how many tables I had already sat at, from the classroom to the boardroom. We move from one table to the next without noticing how each one shapes us. Tables are not just places where people gather. They are places where we learn who we are, who we are becoming, and how to best connect with different types of people.

The Meaning of a Table

Tables are where conversations unfold, decisions are made, hearts connect, and courage grows. A table can represent belonging or distance, listening or dismissal, unity or separation.

Around those early tables, however they looked, we learned something about sharing space with others. Sometimes we were taught to listen. Sometimes we were taught to stay quiet. Sometimes we learned that people could disagree and still return to one another, and other times we learned that was not always the case. All of it shaped us.

As life goes on, we find ourselves at all kinds of tables—boardrooms, conference rooms, client offices, coffee shops, and virtual rooms. Think for a moment about the tables you sit at on a daily or weekly basis. How comfortable is each seat you fill?

I have sat at tables that lifted me up and others that made me question whether my voice mattered. I have watched people shrink themselves to fit in, while others took up more space than they needed. In the early part of my career, I just wanted an invitation to have a seat. As my experience grew, so did the invitations.

Some people are invited simply because their titles look powerful enough on paper, and some are invited because of their bank account or what others assume they have. The truth is, even if you have both the title and the money, that does not guarantee it is the right table. If you have neither, it does not mean you are the wrong person.

There have been moments when I wanted a seat at certain tables and realized my invitation would never arrive because my metrics were not large enough. In some instances, it does not matter how many tables you have built, how many teams you have led, or how much difference you have made. What matters in some rooms is the number of followers, subscribers, and downloads.

I learned this when I reached out to be a guest on someone's podcast to share about this book and the work behind it. I was not asking to be interviewed by Brené Brown, but even if I were, why not, right? Still, the response I received was simple. I did not have enough Instagram followers for my voice to be heard on that podcast.

In that moment, it did not matter that the platforms I had built from nothing had brought together leaders, executives, and changemakers I never imagined sitting with. None of the changemaker guests I interviewed ever asked about metrics. They said yes because of connection, sincerity, and the belief that stories can help others feel seen, supported, and heard. The intention has always been to make a meaningful difference in someone's life. When more than one person is positively impacted, the mission has already exceeded itself.

Those who share their stories do so to serve the listener, to inspire hope, and to lift someone beyond themselves, not for exposure or ego. Yet in this instance, sharing my own story and the reason I do this work, helping others feel empowered to build their own table, became tied to the size of the audience and the ratings I could bring to their show. When that metric was not met, the worth of the message diminished in their eyes, as if impact only holds meaning when validated by numbers.

When you find the right table, the one aligned with your values, you do not shrink; you rise. Trust deepens. Collaboration accelerates. Connection becomes the current that carries the work forward.

Eventually, I learned that some tables are not meant for you, not because you are unworthy, but because they were never built with your kind of truth in mind. When you stop waiting for permission and instead take inventory of the seats you have earned, you may realize it is time to build your own table.

2020: When Life Rearranged the Chairs

In January 2020, my youngest daughter and I moved out of our home of more than twenty years while I juggled three roles: full-time at the New Jersey Business and Industry Association, coaching through Today is the Day LLC, and co-leading the Zzak G. Applaud Our Kids Foundation. I wanted my two passion paths to sustain our life, but they were not there yet, so I carried all three.

Michele Siekerka, NJBIA's president and CEO, is someone I have deeply respected and admired for more than twenty years. Back when I was working with the American Heart Association, she was the president and CEO of the Mercer Regional Chamber of Commerce and served on my executive leadership team for the Mercer County Heart Walk. She fielded a team called Chamber with Heart. We have stayed connected ever since.

I adore and look forward to our continued breakfast catch-up meetings that we have throughout the year. Michele is someone I call for guidance and advice, but she is also someone I am grateful to call a friend. So, when the opportunity came to work for her at the NJBIA, I was thrilled. I proposed and championed creating a Nonprofit Council for the association, and she agreed without hesitation.

Our first meeting was planned for February 2020, with Fred C. Wasiak, former president and CEO of the Food Bank of South Jersey and founder of Humanics Consulting, leading what would become our famous twelve-minute icebreaker. In that short time, he sparked connection, community, and purpose, setting the tone for what the council would grow to represent. None of us knew then that those moments of connection would carry us into one of the most challenging periods we had ever experienced.

Then March arrived. The world changed!

I opened each Zoom meeting with music. It connected us, made us smile, and gave us a moment of lightness we all desperately needed. With Michele leading the way in wanting to support the nonprofit sector, I was responsible for hosting the calls and securing weekly guest speakers. Small things mattered. They helped us remember we were not alone.

By October 2020, shifting models turned my employee role into a consulting engagement. It was humbling, unexpected, and disorienting at first. Yet in hindsight, it became the pivot that opened every door that followed.

The podcast would have remained an outdated dream from 2015 that never happened. The Forum would never have been imagined. And this book would still be a memoir, I believed I should have written years ago, but never did. That one shift created an entire ecosystem. What felt like a disruption was actually the ignition point. It did not just redirect my path; it cleared it. It made way for everything that came next.

Building My Own Tables

The day I was notified that my role would shift, I sat on my couch feeling the weight of an entire year. We had moved out of our home of twenty years. My twenty-three-year relationship had ended. My children were navigating life virtually. The full-time stability I depended on was slipping away. There were many more changes that we were going through as a family at that time.

In that moment of stillness, the podcast idea I once had during my coaching certification came rushing back. Back then, the doubts drowned it out. Who would listen, who would I interview, who would care? I tucked it away because the fear spoke louder than the possibility.

But that day, the idea did not whisper. It pushed. It insisted. It asked me to reconsider what I believed was possible.

Perspective is everything. Mine felt heavy, but I could not ignore the reality that people were doing extraordinary things in the middle of extraordinary hardship. People disliked Zoom, yet Zoom kept us connected. Without it, how would we have supported one another? I thought about the countless people I had met in my career, each carrying powerful stories and lessons that could shift someone else's perspective.

The impact I make through coaching transforms individuals. The impact I could make by creating this podcast had the power to transform communities. I felt called to both.

The problem was that I had no idea how to start a podcast. I knew how to create a YouTube channel, but streaming was something entirely different. Still, something in me refused to let the idea go. I spent countless waking hours thinking of a name for the podcast, learning about streaming, and thinking about what kind of format I wanted for the show. I made mistakes and learned from them. Ironically, I now teach classes on how to do exactly what once felt impossible.

I knew I wanted to interview the inspirers, motivators, and those disrupting the status quo in the best way possible, and suddenly the word, changemaker showed up in my search, and Today is the Day Changemakers was born.

I chose a date ten weeks away and said out loud, I am doing this! There was no question.

I chose December 30 because the new year needed to begin differently.

I have always found that when you put a date on the calendar and take small steps toward it every day, something shifts. I cannot explain why, but goals move closer. Momentum builds. Worry holds you in place. Action moves you forward.

My oldest daughter, Gabriella, helped produce the first season. My now son-in-law, Sean, composed the music. And when I hit publish for the first time, my youngest daughter, Sienna, walked in with a cookie cake and balloons. I love balloons. That moment stays with me. It was a moment of celebration, love, and arrival. After that, Tara Marie Stemkovsky started producing the podcast. She is one of the changemaker authors in this book. Our connection started when we both worked for the American Heart Association.

In the beginning, I watched the metrics the way many podcasters do, wondering if anyone was listening. But I remembered the promise I quietly made to myself when I decided to go forward with this—that if one person was helped, even someone I would never meet, it would be worth it.

The funny thing is that several times while I am at a networking meeting or an event, someone will come up to me and say, "You do not know me. You are Jodi, right? I listen to your podcast." They share how an episode helped them, inspired them, or stayed with them.

Those are the moments when my feet do not touch the floor. Not because of ego, but because a table was built, a guest said yes, and someone from afar pulled up their own chair and joined us, taking in the pieces of the conversation that supported them in their own life.

I invited people whose leadership had inspired and impacted me at different points in my life. My first guest was Michael Weamer, now president and CEO of The Marfan Foundation. It was a full circle moment, especially because I had written about him earlier in the book.

Quickly, as the interviews continued, guests began suggesting others I should interview. Soon, I was speaking with changemakers across the country and beyond. I interviewed a retired four-star US Army General, CNN Heroes, TEDx speakers, celebrity band members, television producers, actors, philanthropists, nonprofit leaders, a former federal agent, people who lead powerful missions of service, executives, creatives, and individuals with deeply personal stories of resilience and transformation. The table kept expanding. Every person who joined brought a new perspective, a new lesson, and a new way to inspire others.

People regularly tell me they share things on my podcast that they do not typically share elsewhere. They say I ask the questions others do not, and I believe that is because I care about the human being behind the work. Their background stories are just as impactful and important as the work they are doing, showcasing how our journeys are never a straight line.

The podcast has now reached listeners in more than 137 countries and over 1,200 cities worldwide and continues to grow.

Every time I sit across from a podcast guest, I find myself asking, "How did I get here"? And I remember the girl who once stayed quiet, unsure, and afraid of being seen, and how finding those who believed in her brought forward a confidence she didn't know she had. That is what connection does.

Decisions That Become Movements

As the interviews continued, I thought about the incredible potential these guests may have if they met one another. They would not typically cross paths, as they were from all over the world. But if we created an online event for meaningful conversations, global connection, and personal and professional development, imagine what could happen. Authentic collaboration. New ideas and opportunities. Connections that could ignite something bigger.

I reached out to many of my guests, and they agreed it was a great idea.

That first year was thrilling. With changemakers from around the globe involved, six breakout sessions planned, and global networking led by Fred C. Wasiak, we were set for success. But what happened next was a perfect example of connection.

I saw online that Henry DeSio Jr. wrote a book, *Changemaker Playbook*. When I looked him up on LinkedIn, I saw that one of my changemakers, a CNN Hero and recipient of multiple awards, was connected to him. I connected with Henry directly, but was not going to immediately ask if he would keynote an event that was brand new.

But that guest introduced us. DeSio, a former White House deputy assistant to President Obama, became the first keynote speaker for the Today is the Day International Changemakers Forum. To say that was a special moment of manifestation is an understatement.

The second year, we had people from twelve countries represented and 150 people in attendance. Stephen M. Cohen, author of *Leading From Within: A Guide to Maximizing Your Effectiveness Through Mediation* and cofounder and chair, Meditation4Leadership, was our keynote speaker. He is also an author in this book. JD Wilson, founder of Lead U and another author in this book, led global networking for two consecutive years.

These yearly connective events bring people together from all backgrounds, and they leave with new connections, a new perspective, and strategies and resources they can use as soon as they close their Zoom room.

A thought became a movement. A movement became an ecosystem. Next, we will celebrate the Today is the Day Changemakers Connective, where you too can have a seat at the table.

Your Invitation

In the pages ahead, you will meet extraordinary individuals who said yes to joining me at a table I built and who have built meaningful tables of their own. Each one is a heart-centered human committed to making a difference in their corner of the world and beyond. Their backgrounds vary, their industries differ, but they are united by a shared devotion to truth, humanity, and lifting others through connection.

This book is a testament to that commitment. It captures their stories, lessons, and lived experiences, and reflects the impact each of us has the opportunity to make when we choose to lead with purpose and heart. Together, we form a connective ecosystem rooted in courage, authenticity, and meaningful change.

As you move through these chapters, allow yourself to slow down and *be fully present* with what you are reading and with the feelings that rise to the surface as you go. Notice what resonates, what nudges you, what expands something inside you, and what invites you to look at your own story differently. Let the Embrace the Moment questions guide you inward, helping you deepen your reflection and consider the steps that may be calling you forward. When you reach the back of the book, spend time in the Meet the Changemakers section to explore each author's work and discover the connections that may support your journey.

Welcome to our table.
Pull up a chair.

LIVE IT!

Embrace the *moment*

We are all everyday changemakers – each of us contains the ability to make an impact in our own way.

What inspires you to be a changemaker?

Jodi invites you to reflect with two additional questions:

When you think about the tables you sit at right now, which ones honor you, make you feel seen and heard, and which ones leave you dreading the moment you have to pull out a chair?

How often do you pause long enough to truly see the person in front of you and feel the connection in that moment? How can you hold yourself accountable moving forward to staying present in your relationships, your leadership, and your life?

Visit the "Meet the Changemakers" section at the back of the book to connect with and learn more about all of the authors featured in **LIVE IT!**

CHAPTER 3

Own Your Voice,

Speak

with Conviction

CHANGEMAKER: CHAYA PAMULA

I dedicate this chapter to my courageous,
kind-hearted mother, Mrs. Vijaya Lakshmi Yerramilly,
whose strength, values, and selfless leadership continue
to inspire my journey and to my daughter Anusha,
whose discipline, kindness, and quiet confidence
inspire me every single day.

"One question asked may change your path;
one question withheld may cost you a destiny."

– CHAYA PAMULA

I was born in a small, modest town in Southern India—one of those places where simplicity is not a lifestyle but a way of being. I came into the world as part of a large, tightly knit family. Our home was always filled with noise, food, laughter, and at times, the quiet tension of survival.

My father was the eldest of his siblings and the backbone of our extended family. As a chief engineer in a sugar factory, he commanded deep respect—not because he demanded it, but because he lived with integrity. He believed in the dignity of hard work and responsibility. I remember how he treated his work like worship and handled family matters with unwavering resolve.

My mother, on the other hand, was the soul of our home. A high school graduate, she might not have held a formal title or degree in leadership—but if life were fair, she'd have won a Compassionate Leadership Lifetime Achievement Award. She managed everything—our household, our finances, and most importantly, our hearts. She taught us that kindness was power and service was strength.

Looking back, I realize I was raised by two leaders—one led with discipline and silent strength, and the other with emotional intelligence and grace. Their actions, more than their words, shaped my values and identity.

The Unthinkable Loss

During my teenage years, I lost both of my parents. I didn't recognize the impact then—grief wasn't immediate, but it deepened slowly over the years. And with it came a silence—an internal one—that made me question whether I could move forward. I felt naive, insecure, and completely unprepared for what life was about to demand of me.

Until then, I had been lovingly sheltered in a family rooted in care and unity. But when that foundation disappeared, I became deeply aware that so many children face similar loss—but without even the early support I had received. That thought never left me.

I knew I couldn't bring back what I lost, but I could become someone I needed—someone who would help children like me. That silence and pain—I chose not to let it define me. I chose to convert my adversity into action.

SOFKIN: A Voice for the Forgotten

That choice took shape in SOFKIN—Support Organization for Kids In Need (www.sofkin.org).

SOFKIN was born from the ache of absence and the fire of purpose. I started it to provide children not just with shelter, but with safety, love, and belief—things I knew were essential because I had once lost them. These children don't just need resources. They need reassurance that they matter. We invest in their education, confidence, and long-term growth.

At SOFKIN, we don't just take care of children—we empower them to discover their voice.

PamTen: Building a Vision Larger Than Myself

As SOFKIN grew, I found myself drawn to building something bigger—something that could extend empowerment into professional spaces. That's when I started PamTen (www.pamten.com).

At first glance, PamTen is a technology company. But its mission is much deeper. PamTen was built as something larger than myself—a company where purpose meets innovation, where culture embraces compassion. PamTen not only supports SOFKIN financially but also offers real-life internships, training, and job opportunities to the very children we raise. It closes the loop—from vulnerability to self-sufficiency.

What began as a business also became a platform to hire, mentor, and develop future changemakers.

SheTek: Amplifying the Voice of Women in Tech

As I navigated the tech industry, I became increasingly aware of how often brilliant women were unheard, unseen, or underestimated. I knew that story well—I had lived it. And I knew something had to change.

So I created SheTek (www.shetek.net).

SheTek was founded to train, mentor, and connect women with the ever-evolving world of technology. It's not just a reskilling program—it's a community. A movement. It helps women claim their space, ask for support, and build resilient, fulfilling careers.

And what makes it even more powerful? Some of the girls from SOFKIN are part of this journey too. They train with SheTek. They are mentored by professionals in the industry. They are being shaped not just into workers—but into leaders.

A Unified Mission, A Natural Connection

SOFKIN, PamTen, and SheTek may seem like separate initiatives—but they are a single story. They are deeply interwoven by one mission:

To empower those who might never otherwise be told, "You can."

SOFKIN nurtures children to rise.

SheTek empowers women to rise, thrive, and lead.

PamTen connects purpose with opportunity by providing funding, mentorship, and opportunities for women and children to thrive and succeed.

I didn't have someone to guide me early on. So I built what I wish I had—organizations born not from strategy decks, but from lived experience, empathy, and deep alignment with my core values.

This is how I create: when I see a gap that holds others back, I build something to bridge it. I use adversity as a blueprint. I use voice as a tool. And I build with conviction.

Grace in Family: Quiet Conviction in Action

In the early years of my marriage, I lived in a joint family, where roles, expectations, and traditions are deeply rooted. It was there that I truly observed how respect is earned over time, not demanded. My mother had set that example, earning her place in a large family by giving more than she asked for, choosing empathy over ego.

I followed her path. I didn't fight for my rights. I didn't make demands. I didn't try to stand out as a threat. I gave my time. I adjusted my priorities. I earned trust. Slowly, through conviction in my intentions and care for the family, my voice began to carry weight. I was heard. I was valued.

As women, we must know when to lean in and when to stand tall. Not every situation needs a loud response—sometimes, it needs presence, persistence, and integrity.

The Power of Support

Behind every voice that rises, there is a strong support system that holds it steady. Mine comes from my husband, Mohan, and my daughter, Anushawho have stood by me as my confidence, inspiration, and support through every bold decision and mission I've pursued.

Alongside them, I've been guided by a circle of mentors who not only advise me but deeply respect the purpose that drives me. Their wisdom and encouragement have been priceless.

I've always believed that we don't climb alone. I've been intentional about building a strong support network—both personally and professionally—because without it, I would not be able to do what I do today. This includes my business partner Prasad, friends & family, employees and clients who have become sponsors, donors and volunteers to my philanthropic endeavors. Every achievement, every voice empowered, stands on the foundation of that collective belief and unwavering presence.

Learning from Bob Proctor: The Inner Shift

I've always believed in manifestation—even before I fully understood it. I've visualized outcomes, declared intentions, and watched them unfold. But this belief became deeply grounded after an unforgettable experience with Bob Proctor, a renowned motivational speaker, author, and success coach best known for his teachings on the power of the mind, self-belief, and the law of attraction. He gained global recognition through *The Secret* and inspired millions to unlock their potential through positive thinking and personal development..

I was invited to an event where Bob Proctor's work was being celebrated. After his keynote, he opened the room for questions. He spoke passionately about desire, belief, and manifesting success. He shared an example: if you want to earn a million dollars, don't see it as one massive goal—break it into ten steps of $100K each and work toward them steadily.

At that moment, I was struggling to raise the final $150,000 to begin construction on SOFKIN's children's home. I raised my hand—not fully knowing what I was going to ask, but knowing I had to speak.

When the microphone reached me, I spoke from the heart. "I live with purpose," I said. "I care for over fifty SOFKIN children living in a small apartment with just one bathroom. I've raised most of what I need, but I'm short $150K to build them a real home. How can you help me?"

Bob was visibly moved. After a pause, he said, "I admire your courage. If you can find fourteen people in this room to give $10,000, I'll be the fifteenth."

I looked around—I didn't know anyone else in the room except the two friends who brought me there. But then he turned to the audience and said, "If you believe in this woman and her noble cause, raise your hand if you'll contribute $10,000."

In thirty seconds, fourteen hands went up.

Bob called me on stage, handed me his check, and said this had never happened in any of his events before. He called it a real-life example of the law of attraction—a response to pure purpose, positive energy, and the courage to ask.

I teared up. I jumped with joy. And I realized something deeper: When your request is genuine and selfless, the universe responds.

Bob told me later, "It was your positive energy that moved that room."

And I never forgot what my mother used to say—"You lose nothing by asking—but you may lose a fortune by not asking."

I was a shy little girl once. But I learned to ask. And every time I did, I strengthened my self-belief and inner confidence.

Takeaways

Self-Belief Fuels Courage: Believing in yourself is the foundation for finding the courage to speak up, even in difficult or uncomfortable situations.

Speaking Up Is a Strength, Not a Weakness: Voicing your thoughts respectfully and assertively shows inner strength and clarity, not defiance or arrogance.

Conviction Commands Respect: When you speak with conviction, people listen—not because you're loud, but because you're clear, authentic, and confident.

Asking for Help Is a Form of Strength: Knowing when to seek support is not a sign of weakness—it's a courageous act that reinforces your self-awareness and resilience.

Every Voice Has the Power to Inspire: Your story, your stand, and your words can empower others to believe in themselves and speak up too—your voice matters.

In Closing

You don't need to be loud to be heard.
You don't need to have it all figured out to start.
You just need to believe enough to take the first step—and to speak, even when your voice shakes. Own your voice. Speak with conviction. Because someone out there is waiting to find their voice through yours.

LIVE IT!
Embrace the *moment*

We are all everyday changemakers – each of us contains the ability to make an impact in our own way.

What inspired Chaya to be a changemaker?

AUTHOR'S REPLY:

What inspires me as a changemaker is the power of connection—linking compassion with opportunity, and purpose with action. Seeing a child thrive, a woman rise in tech, or a career begin because of an ecosystem I helped build reminds me that true impact comes from creating pathways where none existed before.

NOW IT IS YOUR TURN...

What inspires you to be a changemaker?

Chaya invites you to reflect with two additional questions:

When was the last time you truly believed in yourself enough to speak up, even if it felt uncomfortable - and what changed because of it?

Is there a challenge in your life that could be transformed into a mission - something that could empower not just you, but others too?

Visit the "Meet the Changemakers" section at the back of the book to connect with and learn more about all of the authors featured in **LIVE IT!**

CHAPTER 4

I Was Born

Afraid

CHANGEMAKER: AMY DELMAN

Dedicated to my twin sons, Justin and Jake –
who taught me a love I could never have imagined.
They have been a continuous blessing to me all through
life's ups and downs and have shaped every decision
I have made since they were born.

"In my world of media relations, a no today can be a yes tomorrow, and this has become my life's mantra."

— AMY DELMAN

I have no idea why, but from a young age, I always remember being afraid to try new things. Yet, funny enough, when I look back at my life, I have taken so many risks and leaps of faith that have, against all odds, worked out better than ever expected.

Am I still afraid? Yes, every single day. I grew up in a loving household in an affluent New York City suburb with parents who adored me. I made lifelong friends I still have today. My parents encouraged me to push against the limits I placed on myself. For some reason, therapy has never been able to uncover the reasons why I have always been afraid. Afraid to drive alone outside of my geographic comfort zone. Afraid to be judged, afraid of rejection, and the list goes on.

Interestingly, fear motivates me. It gets me to take risks I never would have believed possible. Yet, no matter what, I still experience that pit in my stomach, the feeling I will vomit at any point as I proceed forward with clenched fists, hoping they will allow me to hold onto some kind of stability in in this most unstable world.

As a little girl, I took figure skating lessons. With the instructor, I skated in leaps and bounds within the circles in the middle of the rink, picking up speed, feeling the wind in my hair. As soon as the instructor left, I went back to the wall, terrified to let go for fear I would fall. My mother desperately wanted me to continue skating in the middle of the rink; she knew I had the ability, as she had just watched me do so for an hour with the instructor.

At that rink, they sold the best-smelling French fries. I wasn't allowed to buy these expensive fries. One afternoon, probably frustrated beyond belief, my mother said that if I skated in the middle of the rink without my instructor, she would buy me the fries. So, I skated in the middle of the rink, felt the wind on my face, and the freedom of gliding on ice. I ate the fries victoriously! The next day, I would not go back to skating in the middle of the rink without my instructor by my side. I learned without yet having the words that for me to accomplish my goals, I had to have a reason that was bigger than my fear.

I went away to college about forty-five miles from my home, even though I was accepted into more prestigious schools. I loved living on campus, and I loved knowing that I could be home in less than an hour if I needed to flee. I never needed to flee, but I knew I could. Did going to that college affect my life's long-term goals? I will never know.

Growing up, I went to sleep-away camp, parties, and did all the things my friends did. But I had a secret. If I were with people I knew, I would be fine. If I was alone, I would panic. My husband grew up in a town just a few miles away, and we planned a wonderful future staying close to family and friends. When his job required us to relocate to another state, I did, but I was terrified. I was afraid of being far away from everything and everyone I ever knew. I was less than two hours from where I grew up, but for me, I might as well have been on Mars.

I love structure and planning. I love knowing what my day will bring and being prepared. I was a smoker. I lied to everyone about my smoking because I knew it was wrong. When I became pregnant, I had to fill out a ton of medical forms. I checked the box for non-smokers on each of the forms. Why did the doctor have to know that I was smoking close to a pack a day? During my first appointment, the doctor kept asking over and over about the date of my last period. I repeated it two or three times, then got annoyed. She told me I was pregnant, but she wanted to send me for an eight-week sonogram to get the true gestational age of the baby. Never having been pregnant, I assumed this was standard procedure. All my friends who already had children told me they never had to go for a sonogram that early in their pregnancy. Lo and behold, I found out I was carrying twins. And not just twins, but the highest risk form of identical twins—they were in one sack with one placenta. Should that placenta break, they both would die.

When I went back to see the doctor to discuss next steps, her first words rang in my ears: 'Thank God you are not a smoker.' *Uh-oh*, I thought. 'Why,' I asked. She told me that women who smoked during a high-risk pregnancy ran the risk of pre-term labor, meaning the babies wouldn't be able to breathe on their own or have cerebral palsy or a multitude of other horrifically sounding illnesses, if not death for one or both of them.

Walking out of the doctor's office after that appointment, I threw the pack of cigarettes that were in my purse into the garbage can. I have not smoked since that day. How did I quit a pack-a-day smoking habit? The same way I handle everything else in life--the fear of harming my children was much greater than any pleasure smoking brought me.

My twin sons were full-term and healthy. When they were two, I became sick with a devastating autoimmune disorder. Scary stuff, right? I was not just afraid. I was very afraid. Why? Because my sons deserved a fully active and present mother. I had felt blessed beyond words to have these children, and I couldn't let them down now. I took every treatment and, with clenched fists, moved forward, first with baby steps and setbacks, then baby steps that turned into bigger steps until, years later, they found a medication that could control this illness. Again, words cannot describe how blessed I am to be symptom-free. My fear of being a disabled mom was greater than the fear of trying experimental drugs with sometimes terrible side effects to get better.

I thanked the higher powers that my disease was not hereditary. I could endure being sick, but I could not bear it if my children were.

I am a corporate soldier. For twenty years, I rose up the corporate ladder in companies that couldn't fire me for becoming sick. Not that I ever told them the truth. They knew something was wrong with me, just didn't know what, and couldn't legally ask.

Throughout all this, I continued to work full-time and excel in my career. Having someplace to go and a routine to follow made me feel safe. Even though I was sick, I tried to hide it, and believe me, for the most part, I did. Then my sons became too old for the patchwork of childcare options I had set up for them—from the in-house nannies, to the pre- and after-care programs during school hours, to the babysitters, to the college kids who would drive them and help them with their homework; while I worked sixty-hour weeks safely tucked away in my corporate refuge.

Then came high school and a traumatic downsizing for me. The boys were too old for babysitters, and I no longer had the safety net of my job. I knew I could not go back to corporate America. The hours, the travel, the time spent away from home, and the slim reality of finding a job as someone in her mid-forties.

So, I started my own boutique public relations consultancy. ME? YES, ME! I had never in my wildest dreams had any thought or desire of becoming a solopreneur. I never took any business classes or had any type of business training. This was an option that came to me one day out of the blue.

Of course, I was very afraid! There was no safety net; I had to go out and meet new people and get them to trust me. There wasn't just one boss to please—as a solopreneur, you take whatever work comes your way—so there were many bosses, each with their own style. I was out of my corporate hiding place and in the middle of an unknown reality I knew nothing about. Unbelievably to me, I added one, two, then three clients in under a year! That was almost two decades ago, and my consultancy has grown with now award-winning clients! And I have never looked back!

At the time, I could not believe I was doing this. White knuckled, I moved forward toward a new stability I would have to create. Why? Because the fear of running a business by myself was smaller compared to the risk of having to work for someone else, where I might be downsized again and again.

Then came the divorce. Like the stoic corporate soldier I was born to be, I was also born to be a wife and a mother. I grew up on 'Brenda Bride' books, which my well-meaning grandmother bought me. Brenda was a happy bride, with a perfect husband and a wonderful life. I often wonder if we are doing a disservice to our young girls by perpetuating this fantasy. I have no answer. All I know is that we all learn at some point that Brenda Bride does not really exist.

My parents were married for almost fifty years when my mom passed away. There were some divorces in my family, but the majority stayed together through thick and thin. I never envisioned myself as a divorcée, especially in middle age. I was terrified, but staying and forcing another person to stay in an unfulfilling marriage was not right, nor fair, to either one of us.

I was the one with the illness; he was totally healthy. He had stuck by me throughout and would probably still have if I had not given him permission to go. It was one of the toughest decisions I ever had to make. Now, I really had to skate all by myself in the middle of the ice without any guardrails. If I fell, which I did, I had to pick myself up, which I did. If the business didn't do well, first there was the Great

Recession, and then a global pandemic soon after—it was just me who had to figure out a way for both me and the business to survive.

Sometimes, until we are truly tested, we do not know how much resilience we have. When my mom, who I was extremely close to, was dying, I sat by her side while they were turning off the machines. I held her hand when she took her last breath. I have no idea how I did that or where that inner strength came from. Same with giving up cigarettes. Same with raising twins. Same with getting sick at a young age. Same with starting a business. Same with getting divorced. Same with starting over, time and time again, whether it be a new venture, a new relationship, or a new phase of life.

Am I still afraid? Yes, every single day. This time, that fear is tempered by successes I can reflect on. If I were able to figure it out then, I would figure it out again and again, and so will you! The rewards are always bigger than the fear. So, skate in the middle of the rink, skate with the wind in your hair, and gustily enjoy those fries. Create your own safe reality that works for you. You deserve it!

LIVE IT!

Embrace the *moment*

We are all everyday changemakers – each of us contains the ability to make an impact in our own way.

What inspired Amy to be a changemaker?

AUTHOR'S REPLY:

It was never my intention to become a Changemaker; however, once I realized so many of the lessons I learned, some great, some painful, could be of use to many others, I decided to share. My goal now is to help as many people as I can with my stories, for no matter if we like it or not, every life is filled with change.

NOW IT IS YOUR TURN...

What inspires you to be a changemaker?

Amy invites you to reflect with two additional questions:

Are you feeling afraid, and if so, what are you doing about becoming brave?

What motivates you to succeed, and what barriers might be keeping you from achieving what you truly want?

Visit the "Meet the Changemakers" section at the back of the book to connect with and learn more about all of the authors featured in **LIVE IT!**

CHAPTER 5

How I Got

Here...

The Road Traveled

CHANGEMAKER: DEBORAH KOENIGSBERGER

This chapter is dedicated to my mom,
Curlene Harvey, who taught me everything.

"The day I discovered the meaning of passion was the day my life really began. May each of you follow the path to yours."

– DEBORAH KOENIGSBERGER

From Kingston, Jamaica, to Radio City Music Hall

I was born in Kingston, on the beautiful island of Jamaica, in September 1960. My parents, like most other immigrants before them and since, moved to the United States so that my brother and I could have a brighter future.

The primary reason that they took us, leaving everyone and everything we knew and loved, to settle in a foreign country was to enable us to get an education. Although neither of my parents finished high school, they knew that education was the ultimate "leveler" of the playing field. My brother and I were mandated to prove them right...which we did.

I grew up in a loving community of family and extended family. One for all and all for one was how we lived. Everyone worked hard. My parents did not "preach", instead, they modeled the values and morals I came to adopt. Though they truly only had enough for us, they were extremely generous and charitable. If someone was in need and my parents heard about it, they would swoop in to help.

With this as the backdrop of my childhood, and the understanding that failure was not an option, I started my young adult life with big dreams, after graduating from NYU with a Liberal Arts degree. As a former model turned stylist, I loved everything about the fashion industry and ultimately opened my own French themed boutique, Noir et Blanc in 1989, with the financial support of my parents and a "guardian angel" friend's generosity of heart.

Not long after opening my boutique, which did well right away, three events occurred that ended up defining my life's path.

Event #1: Every day, on my walk to and from work, I crossed Madison Square Park. I was the mother of two young boys, and this park was the closest park to our home. Back then, that park was very unsafe and rundown, yet there was a nineteen-year-old woman and her three-year-old daughter who called it home. They slept in a cardboard box.

Event #2: A chance encounter with makeup artist Bobbi Brown shortly before she took the makeup industry by storm.

Event #3: Seven nights at Radio City Music Hall, third row, dead center, listening to Stevie Wonder's (my absolute addiction of choice) "Conversation Peace" album featuring the song, "Take The Time Out." The lyrics would irrevocably change my life.

The mom and child sleeping on the earth, circa spring 1994.

Incomprehensible. In no world would I have ever been reduced to sleeping on dirt. Someone in the community I was loved by, would have offered a bed...or floor space for me, in the absolute worst of cases. My soul was touched.

After muscling up the courage to approach her, I listened as she told me her heart-wrenching story. She had run away from a physically abusive home environment and gone to a shelter seeking safety and respite. But, she was again violated in the very shelter she had run to for security. She decided to take her chances in the streets. After bringing them food for a few days, they disappeared. Gone. Never to be seen again. I cried for them, and I prayed to God to protect them. Every day as I do this work, I channel them. I imagine them as somehow having been made whole by God's grace. I imagine her daughter as beautiful and strong. I envision them winning all the battles and ultimately the war and living a good life. This prayer keeps me going and has gotten me through many even tougher stories that I have encountered over these thirty-plus years.

The chance encounter.

In the winter of 1994, I was on vacation with my husband and our four-month-old son. Bobbi and I crossed paths in the resort's nursery and exchanged pleasantries. After bumping into each other a second time, we chatted about where we were from and our professions. I was a fairly new small business owner. Bobbi was a budding, super-talented makeup artist waiting for her big break. This break would come merely months after our meeting, and the rest, as they say, is... HER story.

Bobbi offered to visit my store upon returning to New York. After learning about my passion for styling and fashion, she invited me to collaborate with her. For some time, she had been visiting shelters as a volunteer, making up the moms and giving them products. She thought it would be a great idea for me to come along and give the moms a tutorial on how to "dress for success." Our collaborations were hugely successful.

As it turned out, one shelter was located directly between my home and my boutique. I'd previously had no knowledge of "shelter life." Upon arriving, the director met with us and explained how it all worked. She was grateful for the time we took to show these moms love and I was blown away that this existed only blocks away from where I called home. During the event, I noticed that several moms had small children with them, and learned more about the circumstances that brought them to the shelter...Again, my soul was moved.

My addiction.

Growing up, I was crazy about music. There was always music in our home. My mom had a beautiful voice and was always singing or humming a tune. My brother worked in a record store and would bring home the latest records and LP'S. I used to sit by the speakers and play the songs I loved over and over, until I had written down and memorized all the lyrics. My mom would often be heard telling me to STOP scratching the records!

My favorite was Stevie Wonder. Somehow, and I don't know why, at such a young age, I heard Stevie's message. His music made my heart and soul joyous! I grew to love Stevie more and more. As I got older, and began earning my own money, I attended every performance of his that I could. Whenever he played for seven nights (as he normally would), I slept on the sidewalk on my portable beach chair, right beside the scalpers so I could get the BEST seats at box office prices for all seven nights. I lived for Stevie Wonder's words. I was hopelessly and unapologetically addicted. He became my drug. His words became my motivation. His voice soothed me. His lyrics made me feel. His sensibility and deep humanity captivated me, my spirit, and my entire being. There were no bad days that Stevie's words couldn't make better. When I was drowning in sorrow because life would happen, as it did and does to us all, Stevie—a.k.a. solace—was and is always just a click of a button away.

In 1995, when Stevie released "Conversation Peace" and performed for seven nights at Radio City Music Hall, I was in the house; each night, third row center, having "scalped" my own tickets. Once again, for seven magical nights, I was enthralled. One particular song, "Take the Time Out," buzzed in my head, reverberated in my heart, and swept me away. The lyrics held me spellbound in the most beautifully haunting way. It was Stevie. Of course, the message was crystal clear to me. It was yet another message of love. Another thoughtful tutorial on caring, sharing, and taking care of our fellow humans... all of them... not just the "kings" but also the homeless ones. We all need love. Bottom line. "We all play a part in each other's existence," goes the lyrics. Undeniable truths. More raw, powerful Stevie-isms. At one concert, I rushed the stage and kissed him. A highlight of my life! As this song played over and over in my head in the months ahead, I decided that it was written to motivate me to do something... so I did. I looked for opportunities to give back to my community and soon found answers.

The young mother, the Bobbi encounter, and Stevie's words. The "trifecta effect" took a hold of me. It all made sense. It seemed that this was what my parents had been grooming me for my whole life. I felt at the same time "called and assigned." There was peace in that, so I founded the nonprofit Hearts of Gold.

Since then, thirty-one years ago, I have never doubted my purpose. We have advocated for and touched the lives of more than 40,000 homeless mothers and their children through our nonprofit. When I started this journey, I never imagined it would lead here. I just knew I had found my passion... or had it found me?

Hearts of Gold's mission and purpose are audacious. We meet a mom where she is on her journey, and help her to overcome her demons, big or small. We help her to understand that this is not a place to rest her head, but rather just a moment. We all have them. Life, while full of challenges, also brings us an unlimited number of amazing opportunities, if only we take a minute to exhale, to reflect on all that is possible, and to understand that it's all about the journey rather than the destination.

I have met some incredible humans without whom this dream would have remained exactly that... a dream, unrealized. Everything begins with a first step. I often tell the moms and children that dreams come true if you invest your heart in them. While I believe that dreaming big is incredibly powerful, I also know that realizing small dreams pushes us and, in so doing, gives us the confidence and mental readiness to continue to dream even bigger.

When I think of dreaming, it's not a fuzzy, out-of-focus image; it's sharp... it feels almost magical. The thing is to keep that image at the forefront of our minds and not allow life's noises to knock us off course.

When I was twenty, I traveled to Europe for the first time with two college friends. What a life-altering experience! Armed with our back-in-the-day Euro-Rail passes, we traveled to England, Holland, Spain, and France. My major in college was French and Italian literature and language. Since my two friends spoke Spanish and one was fluent in Italian, we were ready for anything...or so we thought. During the trip, we experienced places like Granada, where we discovered the glorious Alhambra, Amsterdam, with its magnificent tulips in full bloom, along with those famous canals, not to be outdone by our stop in the South of France's Cassis, where we all took in a bit too much sun! The "so we thought" part is its own tale. That trip would end up playing a pivotal role in how I would see and understand my life's purpose.

I never set out to be a change agent. I didn't even know what that was. I only knew that, as the starfish story goes, everyone saved is impactful. I have been truly blessed. It all started with my mom and dad, who taught me everything. I married an incredible man, and together we have two awesome, inspiring, generous sons and a boatload of folks who believe in me and support me at every turn. Sharing what I have been lucky enough to receive is fitting. I am full of gratitude and my heart is filled with beautiful lyrics.

Thank you Stevie Wonder! Your vision of what the world could be is imprinted on my soul, as I continue to dream big and fight for a better life for some truly deserving moms and children. Just like my parents did for my brother and me.

LIVE IT!
Embrace the *moment*

We are all everyday changemakers – each of us contains the ability to make an impact in our own way.

What inspired Deborah to be a changemaker?

AUTHOR'S REPLY:

I am inspired by the golden rule, "do unto others as you would have them do to you." When I came to understand the power of one human to impact another's life, I understood the reason for my own existence.

NOW IT IS YOUR TURN...

What inspires you to be a changemaker?

Deborah invites you to reflect with two additional questions:

What is it that stops you from having the life you really want to have?

Do you understand the incredible power you have to effect positive change?

Visit the "Meet the Changemakers" section at the back of the book to connect with and learn more about all of the authors featured in **LIVE IT!**

CHAPTER 6

Eeny, Meeny, Miny, Moe... Finding the Words in the Face of

Challenge

CHANGEMAKER: HEATHER MCCULLOCH

For my son, Aidan, whose resilience and compassion never cease to amaze me, and my husband, Jason, who shows me kindness, acceptance, and love every day. And for my family and friends who held on tight when I needed them most.

"Just because you are right doesn't mean the other person is wrong. You just haven't experienced life while wearing their shoes."

– HEATHER MCCULLOCH

*E*ven though it has been over forty years since I stood near a piano following the lead of my beloved Sunday School teacher, Mrs. Gillen, listening to hymns like "This is My Story. This is My Song," I can still remember how I felt, and I can still remember how bright and ever-present her smile was. It was that kind of smile that made you feel safe, warm, and loved all at once.

I was always the last in line because of my stature, and I was excellent at showing off my eyelids or smiling to make others happy.

Even though I was the shortest—a trend that continued until the summer after ninth grade, when I grew over three inches—I felt like I could conquer the world if only I listened to the words and direction of Mrs. Gillen, a name I struggled to enunciate because of my minor speech impediment and overriding penchant to be intensely shy.

Alas, as soon as I left that room filled with artwork, crumbs from the morning snack, children's Bibles, and the remains of a bobbing for apples game from the night before—yes, churches didn't worry too much about hygiene in those days, I felt small again. The world outside those walls was a whole lot more complicated and at times scary.

As I matured, I continued to latch onto teachers, friends, and others as leaders for me to follow. The thought of leading was too scary. I couldn't imagine entering a figurative dark tunnel, void of any lights. Deep, deep down in my brain, I dreamed of wild adventures and lofty goals, but they stayed right there, buried by my lack of self-esteem and layers of excuses for why I couldn't pursue them.

I slowly learned to step outside my comfort zone once in a while, using that courage that was buried deep in my mind, but for the most part, I was still a card-carrying follower who never dared to cause any waves. In fact, in junior high school, my only claim to fame was being named "The Nicest" when we graduated eighth grade. Ugh, how boring.

I carried on that way for quite a while, sailing underneath the radar, trying not to make too much noise and smiling even when I was hurting or trembling with fear. I excelled in school and landed at a good university where I discovered new things, including my courage and borderline warped sense of humor. My best friend, Mari, was all too willing to take on the challenge of a good Truth or Dare game at any moment. She was also good at bringing out my goofy side and challenging me to step outside my comfort zone until her untimely death following a car accident when we were only twenty-three.

With her encouragement and taking small chances with my eyes closed, figuratively speaking and at times also literally speaking, I learned that inching past the steely boundaries I had made for myself wasn't catastrophic after all. Turned out that the world didn't end, and I still had all my limbs. The realization that doing so could open up so many more opportunities to help others while also making me a little more confident enticed me further.

So, I was that idealistic twenty-something (disclaimer: I still have quite a bit of idealistic thought, and no, I don't think that's a bad thing), and it was full steam ahead as I launched my career as a journalist—no one was going to stop me in my path that I had designed.

My head was down as I plowed forward in a quest to reach my goals. This plight led me, before I turned thirty, to becoming a managing editor at a publishing company and then a journalist at Reuters in New York City, where I later helped to form the new "Power" desk, a.k.a. electricity when that market boomed. Everything was going according to plan...for a little while.

Interspersed were beautiful moments like the birth of my son, which, of course, also led me to make some changes.

One big one was making the decision not to go back to my job in New York City following Aidan's birth so that I could go full force into motherhood and work instead from home on my writing. It just so happened to be 2000, months before 9/11, so I wasn't working in the city when tragedy struck so many, including some of those people with whom I used to commute on the ferry.

Hello reality, those unexpected events that you have no control over. It's amazing how those seem to become more amplified as you age.

My life swerved, and I soon found myself devising ways to make it over obstacles and making that left turn when I needed to. I found myself in a marriage that called for damage control many days and a mask so thick that others knew nothing about what was going on inside the walls of my house and my head. I became a master at numbing my feelings and protecting my child... or so I thought... from seeing anything ugly. I lived that numb-yourself-til-you-don't-feel-anything life for a long time. It worked... or so I thought, using an unhealthy mind. I made excuses, accepted empty apologies from someone who was sick, because on some level, I thought it would work. Like many women, I am a people pleaser.

Huddled behind a locked bathroom door, cleaning up shards of glass from a broken window or picture frame, reconnecting my car's battery, trying to make it through a day after a night of no sleep or filing a missing person's report as quickly as I could so that I could get to a conclusion left me as a facade of who I really was most of the time.

Hidden behind that facade was also an intricate filtration system, of which some of its layers rival the strength of Teflon or the willfulness and steely stubbornness of my second-grade teacher with silvery hair to match. And it wasn't necessarily pretty all the time, either. Sometimes, okay often, it was awkward or so thick that it prevented me from being the person I was meant to be, other times layered with a thick swath of sarcasm. Some tried to poke at it, some poking harder than others, but most were unsuccessful in penetrating the steel. Each dimple in the steel seemed to reinforce its strength but dull its finish.

I say all this because one of the good things about getting older is, dare I say, wisdom - applying what you have learned to deal with those unexpected things in your life and taking notice of those unexpected twists and turns. It's also about recognizing how many things are out of your control... and it turns out that's sometimes a good thing.

About twenty-five years later, and now I look up often on my journey to make sure I'm not missing any unexpected opportunities along the way. I have been doing this for several years, and it has served me well. My son is thriving, and I've met some amazing people and opportunities along the way that I would not have seen had I not looked up.

Despite the ups that turn into downs, my experience has inspired me into thinking that even though something may look impossible, there's always hope; that sometimes no matter how many safety nets you create, things slip through and accidents happen; that trauma can manifest itself in many different ways, often lurking in the dark corners of your journey; that along the circuitous route you often meet people who you would not have met had your course not gone that way; and that no matter how bleak a situation can seem, there is most likely a cracked open door somewhere or one that can be pushed open with a little help.

For several years, I have led Women & Girls Education (WAGE) International, a global nonprofit located in New Jersey that I helped start. We're dedicated to using education to end or prevent violence and abuse against women and girls by mentoring girls and boys to bolster their self-esteem and encourage them to tap into the power they have had all along.

Having fragile self-esteem doesn't mean you are any less intelligent, compassionate, brave, or powerful. It just means that for some, there are many things that block the way of a healthy self-esteem—the cobwebs of the past, the scars that strangle, the negative rhetoric that pervades our world lately. And to foster or rebuild self-esteem on your own is hard. It's an uphill battle that sometimes gets put on hold when life gets in the way.

Through our mentoring, we let kids know that they are not alone, no matter how isolating self-doubt can sometimes seem. They all matter.

In 2025, we launched Global Pen Pals for Peace, in part to encourage more communication and the realization that, in spite of different cultures, our similarities outnumber differences.

It's a bird. It's a plane. It's an opportunity!

Those unexpected events seem to propagate as you age... or maybe it's just that we notice them more often. I'm not advocating that your life takes lots of turns, but I do recommend that you look up once in a while to check out the scenery.

Who knows what you'll find, or what you'll see land in your lap!

Spend less time worrying about people liking you and spend more energy making sure you have the space to express who you really are. You deserve every part of you to be seen and heard. As do others.

My only recommendation would be to pause first so you can assess the room before speaking out loud.

Silence really can be golden. Without the clutter that noise can bring—yes, even the most profound words are still noise, your thoughts are able to flow freely.

In South Korean tradition, the practice of "assessing the room first" is known as nunchi, which literally means "eye measure." It's about checking out the tone, body language, and context of others. This emotional intelligence is a key aspect of Korean culture and can be especially crucial for children in learning empathy, and that "it's not all about you."

Over the years, I have learned that sharing your story isn't always easy, that the fear of pain can sometimes outweigh the impact it may make on others, and that opening our hearts and minds may not always be the best solution for growth. I learned that people are struggling in so many ways. That timing really is everything, and that rejecting the idea that you are a victim can be pretty good for the soul.

I learned that I need to listen even more. I've always been a pretty good listener, but probably mostly because I didn't like to speak up; filling the void with quiet time seemed like the safer choice. Now I listen with intention, with compassion, with no agenda. There's not always an answer. There's not always a solution. Sometimes people just need to know that they are being heard. That validation can go a long way.

I have learned that the life plan often takes a circuitous route and needs to be adapted when some things occur that you weren't expecting, and that sometimes a whole different direction needs to be taken.

In those darkest moments in our lives, it may seem as though there is no way out, or it may seem just too scary to travel down that dark path, but those glimmers of hope tucked in the caverns of that dark path can sometimes be enough to guide us into the light and a brighter future.

Finally, here are some lessons I learned while traveling in Ireland, my family's homeland:

1. Be kinder and more patient.
2. Smile more and laugh a lot.
3. Be responsible... for myself, others, the environment, and my words.
4. Say "fer feck sake" when warranted because a profane word not directed at someone isn't the end of the world, but one unkind act can be. Plus, it can help to release frustration.
5. Pick up trash when you see it... even if it's not yours.
6. Realize that being American doesn't automatically make you more special.
7. Have dessert and a wee bit of Guinness (preferably in Ireland because it's tastier)—it's good for your iron levels and your soul.
8. Don't take life too seriously.
9. Dogs can be windows to our souls.

10. Humility and gratitude can be powerful. Realize that you are a speck in an enormous universe. This doesn't mean that you can't be powerful, capable of doing amazing things. It just means you're only one teeny piece of a much larger pie. Sorry, lad.

11. Stop lumping people into one group. We all belong to many different groups, some of which overlap.

12. Spend less. Give more.

13. Stop rushing. Time rushes forward fast enough—you don't need to speed it up.

14. Listening to good music and reading good literature can go a long way in your pursuit of happiness.

15. Dance even if you have absolutely no rhythm. Yes, you know who you are.

16. Speak with an Irish accent...it's hard not to smile when you do.

17. It matters more what you do on your journey than what you drive.

18. Love more. Hate less. Consider disliking the things people do rather than who they are.

19. Speak up when you think something is unjust.

20. Conformity sucks. Embrace who you are, not what a bunch of other people are.

21. Spend more time speaking with strangers. Listen more.

22. Appreciate natural beauty. There's a lot of it.

23. Even people from different backgrounds and different beliefs can agree sometimes.

24. Swimming in cold water can be good for you....one of these days I'll try it.

25. There's still much to learn...and I can't wait to explore it.

And remember, your journey, no matter what it looks like, was always something that mattered and still does.

LIVE IT!

Embrace the *moment*

We are all everyday changemakers – each of us contains the ability to make an impact in our own way.

What inspired Heather to be a changemaker?

AUTHOR'S REPLY:
My aim is to be a helper, and that means leaving less space for pride and more space for humility and an open heart. It's a privilege to be a light that helps guide a student down the dark tunnel that may be their future.

NOW IT IS YOUR TURN...

What inspires you to be a changemaker?

Heather invites you to reflect with two additional questions:

After reading my chapter, what is the first thing you're going to accept about yourself?

How are you going to make space for someone else's voice?

Visit the "Meet the Changemakers" section at the back of the book to connect with and learn more about all of the authors featured in **LIVE IT!**

LIVE IT! *reflection*

Press Play: The Power of Play-Based Leadership

"Play isn't the break from the work—it is the work."

– JD WILSON

Before any game I played growing up, my mom never asked if we won. She asked, "Did you have fun?" At the time, I didn't realize what she was really asking. Did you press play? Did you show up fully? Did you feel something real while doing it?

As kids, there is an unspoken intuition to press play, to leap, to laugh, to lead without overthinking. That intuition does not disappear with age. It gets buried, distracted, replaced with responsibilities and roles, but it is still there. The definition of play may change over time, but the need for it never does.

As adults, we often forget to press play. We enter performance mode, chasing outcomes, managing impressions, and holding our breath. But pressing play is more than allowing joy. It is the moment we activate our mind, our breath, our body. It is presence. It is courage. It is the starting point for real leadership.

Whatever you are working on creatively, through emotionally, or toward spiritually, my suggestion is simple. Lead with play. Play disarms fear. It builds trust. It creates safety and makes space for others to try again. When we begin with play, we lead not with perfection, but with presence.

So, before you lead, before you fix, before you push, pause... and press play. And maybe, at the end of it all, the most important question to ask yourself isn't "Did I get it right?"

It's the same one my mom always asked: Did you have fun?

JD invites you to reflect on these two questions:

Where in your life have you stopped playing, and how can you start again?

What would happen if you led your team the way you led your playground?

Visit the "Meet the Changemakers" section at the back of the book to connect with and learn more about all of the authors featured in **LIVE IT!**

CHAPTER 7

The Silence

That Shaped Me

CHANGEMAKER: DEBORAH BAKER

To my sons, thank you for being my reason to heal, to grow, and to keep moving forward. To my grandchildren, may you always stand in your truth, speak with courage, and never shrink to make others comfortable. To every woman who has ever felt invisible, unheard, or forgotten, this is for you.

"In the echoes of silence, I found my voice, where pain became purpose and silence became strength."

– DEBORAH BAKER

For years, I carried a silence so loud it echoed in every corner of my being.

I share this now because I know I'm not alone. Too many women, **Sisters in Service,** have carried these invisible wounds, trained to serve, trained to lead, but never taught how to heal. We've suffered in silence, behind the titles, the uniforms, the expectations, but know silence is not strength, nor is it healing. The *Transformation* begins with speaking the *Truth*.

This is not just a story of pain; it's a reclaiming of power. A shedding of what was never ours to carry. A declaration: I will no longer protect the silence or the systems that did not protect me.

I've held on to the secrets of my past for so many reasons, none of which make any sense today. I was around ten or eleven when my world shifted. The abuse wasn't a one-time incident; it was repeated, terrifying, and shrouded in shame. I was told not to tell, but deep inside I needed to. When I finally told a family member that I was molested, I was not believed or protected and was labeled as being "fast." As if my innocence could be mistaken for something I never even understood.

That day, the silence won. I learned my voice didn't matter. I buried my pain beneath a smile and a rebellious streak, hoping someone would see me, but no matter what I did, silence followed. I searched for worth in all the wrong places, thinking: *If I'm lovable enough, loud enough, bold enough, maybe someone will finally see me.*

But no matter what I did, the silence remained.

That mindset and those lies that followed me into womanhood always reminded me, "you're not worthy," "it's your fault," and "you're too much."

Then came the military.

Joining the military gave me identity and purpose. I wore the uniform with pride, but trauma followed me. I became a victim of **military sexual trauma (MST),** and again I stayed silent, conditioned to believe compliance was safer than confrontation.

When I spoke up, I was silenced by the very system I had sworn to serve. My truth was not met with justice or protection but with cold indifference. No one checked on me, and no one stood beside me. The self-blame returned: Maybe it was my fault, I shouldn't have been there, I deserved it. No one acknowledged what I had endured.

Just like in childhood, I wasn't met with care or support but dismissed. I felt ostracized, stayed silent, and once again, left to **suffer in silence**.

You isolate yourself and pretend you're fine. You wear the uniform, move through the motions, and bury the truth, especially when the one who violated you walks by with a smug smirk, as if your pain meant nothing. His silent taunt, "I told you so," echoes louder than words. You lower your head, not out of guilt, but out of the shame you were made to carry, as if it was all your fault.

You keep breathing. You keep showing up, but inside, you're screaming. You feel...

**Invisible – erased in places where I should have mattered
Unheard – speaking truth, but no one listened
Unseen – surviving without acknowledgment of my strength or my pain**

Reset: Acknowledging the Past

Healing starts with honesty, with remembering, feeling, and releasing.

Ask yourself:

- When did I feel silenced?
- What emotions am I still holding on to?
- What would I tell my younger self who thought it was her fault?

Breaking Silence: A Journey of Healing

I moved forward, but not really, functioned, and succeeded. I looked strong on the outside, and inside, I was quietly unraveling. Although I've learned to hide the pain for many years, I now know it showed up in many other areas of my **LIFE**.

To this day, I struggle to let people get close to me. That's the thing about trauma; it doesn't disappear just because you pretend it never happened. It buries itself and shows up in your relationships, self-talk, and sleep. It teaches you to build walls, not trust. It takes you back to the place of "yesteryear," to the familiar ache of being **unseen,** **unheard,** and **unwanted**. For a long time, **I believed I deserved it.**

That's the cruelest part of shame: it convinces us we're to blame, and we are broken beyond repair. What I know today is silence isn't survival it's suffocation.

I was tired of holding my breath; I've held my breath for far too long. Today I am breathing!

I tell my story because **healing begins with truth**. Today, I stand in my **TRUTH,** and when this happened to me, I stood **ALONE**, trying to figure out the **WHY** in this craziness. Today, the weight of yesterday no longer defines who I am; it fuels the mission for which I stand. I speak not just for myself, but for every woman who has **suffered in silence** and continues to stay in that place where you **feel trapped.** For every woman who has masked her pain behind resilience, who deserves to reclaim her voice, I say **start that new journey today**.

Breaking the silence isn't easy. It means confronting the past and finding the courage to name the wound and allowing yourself the grace to heal. I believe that through vulnerability, through shared experience, and through the power of community, **we can step into healing, not alone, but together**.

This is my truth. This is my mission, and the beginning of a movement where no woman walks the path of healing in isolation. **Most importantly, no woman walks alone!**

Reframe: Seeing Yourself Differently

To reframe is to shift perspective, from shame to strength. **Reflect on this:**

- How has your past shaped your strength?
- How would you rewrite your life's narrative?
- What beliefs are you ready to let go of?

For years, I wore the mask of strength, polished, responsible, unshaken, while silence, shame, and survival stormed beneath. It was safer to hide than to be seen, because vulnerability invited punishment and pain risked rejection. I smiled through invisibility, believing the mask was protection, when it was really a facade.

Strength is not the absence of pain. It's the courage to face it.

Taking off the mask was the beginning of real healing, and it didn't happen all at once. It began with **RESET**, a disruption of the lies believed about who I had become. Then came the **REFRAME**, knowing I was not weak, but scared, I now know my survival was not shameful, and I've **RECLAIMED** my journey. I took my power back, not from people, but from the fear, lies, and guilt that kept me small. **I reclaimed my voice. My mission. Myself. It was not easy; it's never been easy. I had to have faith over fear; FAITH moves us forward, and fear keeps us paralyzed. I chose FAITH.**

Healing is never just personal. It's when one woman finds her voice that she gives others permission to find theirs.

When one survivor chooses to lead, she lights the way for those still trapped in the dark.

My healing became my mission. My mission became a movement.

What began as reclaiming my own life evolved into **Sisters in Service, Suffering in Silence** a call to women everywhere:

To Stop Hiding - To Stop Hurting alone - Step into Healing -To Lead -To rise TOGETHER

When one woman rises, she lifts an entire community, and that community lights the path for the next.

You can't heal what you refuse to confront. For a long time, I avoided therapy and went through the motions, making excuses, telling myself I was fine, but surviving is not the same as healing. When I shared my story with my sons, they kindly said what I needed to hear: "Mom, you should talk to

someone." Too often, we settle for surface-level comfort, temporary fixes, feel-good moments, or silent endurance, because diving deeper feels too painful. Know that true healing doesn't live on the surface; it lives at the root, buried beneath the pain, the silence, and the shame. **I cannot change what others didn't do for me, but I can choose how the pain shapes me going forward.**

Call to Leadership

This is my story, and yes, it's painful, but it's also a powerful one. Not because of what happened, but because of what I chose to do with it. **I faced it. I named it. I sought help.** In doing so, I reclaimed the parts of me I thought were lost. I'm a work in progress, but we all are.

To every woman reading this: **Your story matters. Your healing matters. YOU MATTER!**

Lead your own journey - Don't wait for permission - Be the woman who says, **"This ends with me."**

You don't have to be perfect; you must be willing. There is power within you, and the world needs that power now more than ever. **Reset your story. Reframe your truth. Reclaim your power.**

To the woman still wearing the mask: *you are not alone.*
To the woman silencing her truth: *your voice is powerful.*
To the woman wondering if her story matters: *it absolutely does.*

There is space at this table for your truth.
There is healing not in isolation, but in community. You were not meant to stay hidden.
You were born to reset, reframe, and reclaim.

A Life of Purpose

Healing isn't just about feeling better. It's about becoming better, stronger, and more rooted in who you were always meant to be. When we do the deep work, when we choose truth over silence and growth over survival, we don't just heal for ourselves, we heal forward. We set a new standard for what it means to **live a life of purpose**.

Purpose isn't found in perfection. It's found in the courage to keep going. To get back up and to tell your story and to lead with authenticity and compassion. I now understand that my healing was never just for me; it was for the women coming behind and beside me. This is for every sister who still feels **unseen** or **unheard**, every woman who is continuing to **suffer in silence.**

A life of purpose is one lived fully, truthfully, and unapologetically. It's about taking what was meant to break you and building something powerful with it. It begins the moment you decide:

I will no longer live beneath my potential. I will lead, heal, and will rise on purpose. When I look back now, on the silence, shame, and pain, I no longer see a broken past but a sacred path.

I chose to use what tried to destroy me, not as a weapon, but as a foundation. To build healing spaces, bridges, and a legacy for other women.

My journey is not in vain and neither is yours. I broke my silence so you could feel less alone in yours. You are not what happened to you, but you can choose to:

- Begin again and know you're not alone
- Rise with intention and know your voice matters
- Lead with love and live with purpose
- Always know that healing is possible

Reset your story. Reframe your truth. Reclaim your power.

You deserve every ounce of peace, every breath of freedom, and every moment of joy.

While those lingering thoughts try to creep in, you've already won because you actively choose every day to reset and to fight back against those shadows. You are beautiful. You are bold. And you deserve better.

Your healing is waiting, and so is the *sister* beside you.

Let's rise together. RECLAIM: A Personal Call to Action

You've made it through the silence. You've reframed your story. Now reclaim what is already yours.

- What does reclaiming your power look like?
- How do I define resilience?
- What can I do today to step into the person I am becoming?

LIVE IT!
Embrace the *moment*

We are all everyday changemakers – each of us contains the ability to make an impact in our own way.

What inspires Deborah to be a changemaker?

AUTHOR'S REPLY:

The silence I once carried became the power I now lead with. As a woman, a veteran, and a survivor, I know what it means to be unseen and underestimated. That's why I help women reset, reframe, and reclaim their next chapter. For every woman who's questioned her worth or voice, I'm here to remind her: you are more than enough.

Change is my calling because when women rise, lead, and speak their truth, the world shifts.

NOW IT IS YOUR TURN...

What inspires you to be a changemaker?

Deborah invites you to reflect with two additional questions:

What part of yourself have you hidden to survive, and what part are you now ready to reclaim?

How has breaking your silence led to healing or empowerment in your journey?

Visit the "Meet the Changemakers" section at the back of the book to connect with and learn more about all of the authors featured in **LIVE IT!**

CHAPTER 8

and Found

CHANGEMAKER: LENNY DAVE

To my children, Dena and Avi...and to those whom they
will inspire – from generation to generation.

"Life is a gravy sandwich!"

– LENNY DAVE

*I*f only Life could present us with unmistakable signals, an impossible-to-miss "heads up" notification to pay attention to a special, significant moment that was just about to present itself.

Maybe those signals could be visual, featuring brightly colored flashing lights like the ones that make our heart rate suddenly increase and our brains shift into deflated, panic mode the instant we see them in our rearview mirror as we're driving, oh, a few miles over the speed limit. Would those signals be enough to grab our attention?

Or, maybe that visual signal needs to be accompanied by those instantly recognizable sounds we hear at a railroad crossing. First would be the incessantly pounding ding-ding-ding-ding of the warning bell. Not far behind would be the ever-increasing volume of the blare of the warning whistle from the rapidly approaching train.

But, wait – if the crossing gates are still upright, and if our risk-taking calculations are correct, we're most likely thinking, "I can do this – I can beat that train and avoid an aggravating four-minute delay in reaching my nondescript, uneventful destination."

If only Life could make those special moments simply impossible for us to miss. I wonder, though, even with such dramatic notice, would we really pay any more attention? Or, would we still be just as distracted, disconnected, and disengaged as we routinely go about our business, our well-rehearsed daily routine?

In these significant moments, Life has an uncanny way of teaching us lessons that no conventional classroom could ever convey, not even in the most comprehensive curriculum. No gray-haired professor, no fresh-faced graduate student could ever explain it more clearly and powerfully than our own collection of day-to-day experiences does. Our secret stash of Life's meaningful moments has etched their messages into our consciousness. Sometimes, they have implanted themselves on a much deeper level.

Recognizing, accepting, and learning from these moments only happens when we, ever the student, are ready and receptive. I'm reminded of the popular proverb, "When the student is ready, the teacher will appear." Often, though, the student is not ready, and the decisive moment of learning or enlightenment is lost. My questions to you are simple. Are you ready? Do you pay attention to the signals? Are you aware and present? Do you see and not just look? Do you listen and not just hear? Are you appreciative and grateful?

One of my favorite audiences these days consists of seniors. No, not high school or college seniors. I'm referring to active senior adults, the "fifty-five plus" crowd. However, that generic, demographic label is simply too broad. You see, some seniors are on the go-go-go; some seniors are, quite frankly, nearly gone. The Almighty doesn't play favorites.

Some recent retirees and their significant others still play tennis or golf, go to the theater and the symphony, dine in fine restaurants, delight in creating in the kitchen, work in the garden, play bridge, play mahjong, and still drive their car from here to there without a care. These seniors have found that Life, even with all its medicated aches and pains, isn't so bad. It sure beats the alternative.

By contrast, other seniors are alone, literally and/or figuratively. Perhaps they have lost their beloved soul mate. Perhaps they are losing them now, watching them slip away. Some seniors' mobility is now aided by canes and walkers (yes, the ones with the brightly colored tennis balls covering the base of the metal feet). Some seniors drive electric scooters like Mario Andretti and are hell-bent on getting to wherever they're going – "Beep-Beep!" Some seniors are now dependent on wheelchairs and an ever-present aide who sits with them, helps them move from room to room, takes them to daily social activities and to the dining room...or to the doctor. Their days of living independently have long since passed. They realize that waking up tomorrow is not guaranteed. And for many, their empty facial expression reflects this realization.

I interact with my senior audiences at various stages along their geriatric journey. For some in my audience, their eyesight may have diminished, but their broader vision has been sharpened by their collective years of experience; wisdom that comes with age. What really matters to them is now clearly in focus.

Above all, what I have learned from interacting with my senior audiences is an expansive sense of empathy and compassion. As a comedy historian (not a comedian), in sharing countless, nostalgic memories of the great comedians who have made them laugh for decades, my intention is to create a positive, emotional, shared experience for them.

Prescribed medications may relieve or lessen their physical pain, but humor and laughter provide a free, healthy dose of joy; a booster shot of happiness. Norman Cousins, author of *Anatomy of an Illness as Perceived by the Patient,* said it best: "The more laughter there is, the higher the quality of life. The higher the quality of life, the greater the will to live."

Seeing and hearing about Charlie Chaplin, Lucy, Laurel & Hardy, Jack Benny, Bob Hope, George Burns & Gracie Allen, Milton Berle, Sid Caesar, Red Skelton, Jackie Gleason, Carol Burnett, and so many more never gets old for them... or for me. It always brings a smile to their faces, laughter to their lungs, and happiness to their hearts. I take them back in time so they can recall and relive the past while appreciating it, perhaps even more so, in the present.

On this particular evening several years ago, one of those powerfully memorable Life moments presented itself to me. Fortunately, because my human antennae are always hyper-sensitized before a show, I recognized it and paid special attention.

About fifteen minutes before show time, an aide wheeled an older woman into the theater, carefully positioning her wheelchair in the front row so she could see and hear me better. With the routine delivery completed, the aide quickly disappeared. The woman in the wheelchair wore a heavy, yellow sweater. A scotch plaid blanket covered her legs and torso. But, what struck me as most odd was that she had on a pair of dark, wrap-around sunglasses. Yet, we were indoors and it was evening; the sun had long since set.

Always interested in making the human connection with as many people as possible before a show, I slowly but confidently walked toward the woman and said, "Hello." Then, I noticed it. From whatever medical situation had befallen her (a stroke perhaps, or maybe the latter stages of who knows what), she sat there quiet, motionless, and seemingly non-responsive. She could not move her head; it was tilted slightly back and leaning a bit to the left. She could not move her arms; her left limb lay limp across her lap; her right arm was supported and loosely Velcro-strapped to the wheelchair's armrest.

Let's be honest—at this point, how many speakers and performers would probably have turned away and paid little or no attention to her, if not even outright ignoring her as to not be "distracted" by seeing the difficult situation...and in the front row, no less? Many would probably seek out friendlier faces in the crowd from whom to receive lively feedback during the show.

For whatever reason, at that moment, I chose to do the exact opposite. I moved in even closer, determined to connect with her. As I approached, I smiled and said, "Thank you for coming to my program this evening." When I looked at her eyes through the dark sunglasses, I saw only an expressionless, blank stare; her eyes frozen. I realized this woman was unable to blink regularly, thus the protective sunglasses. In the row behind her, seated maybe ten feet away, a man called out to me in a gravelly New York accent, "She can't talk!" And, for a moment, neither could I.

"What's her name?" I asked with a sense of quiet urgency.

"Barbara," he replied.

I didn't know how long Barbara had been in such a deteriorating medical condition. I also didn't know how many more days Barbara might have had left. Not many, I'm guessing. Regardless, I wanted her to know that, on this night, I was validating her presence, acknowledging that she was still very much a living, human being. She was not just a nameless, faceless, lifeless body in a wheelchair. I put my hand on Barbara's right arm and quietly said, "At the end of the show tonight, I'm going to sing a song for you, no one else—just for you." She said nothing, nor did she move. She couldn't. And, I had no way to know if she even heard my words.

An hour and fifteen minutes later, having playfully taken my audience on a joyful trip down comedy's memory lane, it was time to close the show. What no one but me knew was that I had never sung a song before in any of my shows. It wasn't in the "script," it wasn't in my PowerPoint...and it definitely wasn't in my comfort zone. Sure, I'm an entertaining speaker, but I'm no Tony Bennett—maybe more like Tony the Tiger. Yet, that moment when Barbara was brought into the room had so moved me that I felt this night had to be the night when I just stuck my neck out there and did something extra special and personal for this one woman.

The song I knew I had to sing at that moment was the song most often associated with Charlie Chaplin, "Smile." He wrote the music for it for his 1936 film, *Modern Times*. However, there were no lyrics for the tune until 1954, when the songwriting team of Turner and Parsons submitted something that Chaplin would finally accept. That's why you'll never find a recorded version of "Smile" with lyrics sung prior to 1954. Since then, many great recording artists have knocked out wonderful cover versions of the song. Not on that list, however, was me!

The moment had arrived. There was no turning back. True, the only person in the theater who even knew I had promised to sing a song was one woman—Barbara...and she couldn't talk. Had I closed out the show the way I normally do (with my poem, "Lost and Found"), no one would have ever known any differently.

Forgetting everyone else in the theater, my laser focus was now on this one woman. I walked over to Barbara, knelt down on one knee, and carefully put my left hand on her right hand, holding it gently. My right hand, remarkably steady considering the circumstance, held the microphone. Then, in a hushed tone filled with heartfelt emotion, I began to sing...

Smile, though your heart is aching.
Smile, even though it's breaking.
When there are clouds in the sky,

you'll get by.

If you smile through your fear and sorrow,
Smile—and maybe tomorrow,
You'll see the sun come shining through
for you.

Light up your face with gladness.
Hide every trace of sadness,
Although a tear may be ever so near.

That's the time you must keep on trying.
Smile—what's the use of crying.
You'll find that life is still worthwhile
If you just smile.

When I finished the song, the audience (whom I had blocked out of my mind) applauded in unified, emotional approval. Slowly looking up, I noticed that the man who had earlier told me, "She can't talk," was sobbing uncontrollably and fumbling for his handkerchief to wipe his eyes and blow his nose.

I rose to my feet, leaned over Barbara, gave her a kiss on her right cheek, and then spoke softly into her right ear, "I love you."

Had the story ended there, it would have been memorable enough. What happened next, though, turned out to be one of the most powerful moments of my career. With what very little breath Barbara's lungs could muster, she ever-so-faintly and ever-so-slowly whispered into my right ear, "T—h—a—n—k y—o—u."

I don't know what expression my face showed, but internally I was absolutely stunned. Taking a moment to gather myself, and also allowing the room to catch its breath, I then proceeded to my standard close, sharing excerpts of a particularly personal poem I had written many years ago called "Lost and Found."

You may lose your thinning hair,
And you may lose your hearing.
You may lose your teeth. And ladies,
You may lose an earring.

Laryngitis means you've lost your voice.
The blind have lost their sight.
Some find they see more clearly now,
Knowing everything's all right.

Some seniors lose their license.
But, they haven't lost their drive.
Their wit is sharp, their mind alert.
They're very much alive.

In life, we lose possessions.
But, other "gifts," we find.
To smile despite our challenges—yes,
It's all a state of mind.

So, every day, the choice is yours—
Will you be a doom-and-gloomer?
Buck up, old chum—don't be so glum.
Never lose your sense of humor.

LIVE IT!

Embrace the *moment*

We are all everyday changemakers – each of us contains the ability to make an impact in our own way.

What inspired Lenny to be a changemaker?

AUTHOR'S REPLY:

It's as simple as the fulfillment of creating a sense of community where once there was none. People enter a theater as strangers and leave feeling part of something bigger; I connect the previously disconnected. With humor, by sharing stories and images that awaken long-lost memories or positively shift a mood, my intention is to deliver Happiness—a powerfully visceral and socially contagious feeling. My time-tested tonic is Comedy Nostalgia, blending healthy humor with cognitive stimulation to create emotionally charged moments that resonate deeply. These mirthful moments become even more potent when shared. I'm inspired by the knowledge and confidence that I have this ability to make that impact. As Ethel Merman once said, "If the audience could do any better, they'd be up here on stage and I'd be out there watching them!"

NOW IT IS YOUR TURN...

What inspires you to be a changemaker?

Lenny invites you to reflect with two additional questions:

Of the many people with whom you come in contact, are you willing to connect with one person today? Say "Hello!" or "Thank you!" or "I just wanted you to know that I see how hard you work and I appreciate it." I wonder – what change or reaction might that generate from them? More so, what change might that generate in you?

If there was one person (now departed) to whom you wish you had just one more opportunity to say "thank you" ... or one person with whom you could have just one more meaningful conversation, who would that person be? More importantly, though, is there one person in your world, still among us, to whom the above opportunity might apply? If so, what is keeping you from initiating that communication?

Visit the "Meet the Changemakers" section at the back of the book to connect with and learn more about all of the authors featured in **LIVE IT!**

CHAPTER 9

Crossing
the Widening Gyre

CHANGEMAKER: KATIE MARRA

To my parents: thank you for showing me the
beautiful earth and inspiring me to protect it.

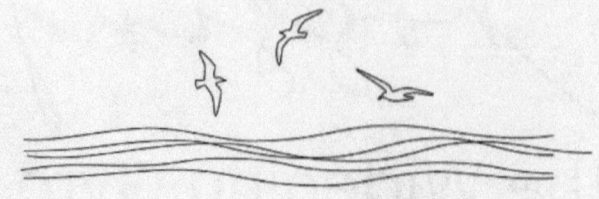

"Do not be afraid, trust your intuition,
and question everything."

– KATIE MARRA

At ten years old, I was lost in the desert. Trudging behind my mom, watching the worried look on her face every time she turned around to make sure a condor hadn't picked me off, I swore I had seen that rock before.

It was evident we were going in circles, and had been for hours, as my dad picked up my heat-stricken five-year-old brother, who had begun babbling delirious nonsense, at least more than usual.

Unsure what to do, we gathered under a large rock, which provided enough shade for two of the children while my dad scouted ahead. With empty water bottles and no sign of the trail we had lost, we discussed the possibility of dying. We had all heard the story of the family who recently died in the area, having gotten lost with no service. They weren't found until it was too late.

My parents were upfront about the severity of the situation; they were not sugarcoating any of it, and it was clear we would all have to contribute to getting out of the predicament we were in. My younger sisters were getting scared. I drew pictures in the sandy dirt, telling them a story to keep them occupied. Through heat-induced brain fog, I made up something hopeful about a lizard finding its way. My youngest sister, who was seven at the time, rose from the shadow of the rock and insisted she knew the way back.

Out of options, we followed her and eventually made our way back to the trail. After we returned to our campsite, I wrote a poem about the desert, including the inspirational lizard.

The summer of 2015 in Joshua Tree National Park shaped my view of the natural world and inspired me to write, learn, and care about it. Getting lost in the desert became more than an indelible memory, but also an allegory for how I see our planet.

At twenty, I realize that we have lost our way, and our future is at risk. Rescue will not come from outside; we must save ourselves, and can only be successful if we work together. The way forward is often marked by the youngest among us.

Narrowly escaping the harrowing situation of being lost in a hostile environment allowed me to realize that human beings' ability to survive in this world is not a foregone conclusion and that life on Earth is dependent on a delicate balance.

Throughout my life, I have been inspired by the natural world, which sustains us, and have become endlessly curious about how we are impacting it. With new respect for the ecosystems around me, I began to study the Barnegat Bay watershed and the wetland ecosystems here in my native New Jersey. While the great national parks of the American West were well-known and appreciated, I found equally important but underappreciated, and in some cases, outright neglected ecosystems in my own backyard.

Growing up in suburban New Jersey, it became clear to me that we must reconnect with nature in a meaningful way. The disconnect from the native landscape is underscored by our computer screensavers of vibrant coral reefs or cascading waterfalls—places far away that govern our understanding of nature. Often, New Jersey practices a profound nimbism for nature, reserving our attention and appreciation for these places.

Meanwhile, we continue to decrease insect populations, pollute the groundwater with lawn fertilizer, and plant our beds with nonnative invasive species. Living in Toms River specifically, the location of two major superfund sites, pollution is a formative element of the town. Through this awareness, I began to see the state of peril the planet is in and have decided to devote my life to understanding the problems that we are facing. I aim to work to develop better solutions to these problems and learn new approaches to communicating to the public in a way that both informs and mobilizes the change our planet needs.

Our global temperature is climbing, ice sheets are shrinking, sea levels are rising, and extreme weather events are increasing in frequency. Our climate is changing rapidly for the worse, and we have everything at stake.

For young people, especially, growing up with the earth in this state is terrifying and heartbreaking, not to mention a huge responsibility to take on.

I cope with this by studying ecology so I can help figure out ways to mitigate the effects of climate change by understanding ecosystem responses. Specifically, I am studying native bee populations in urban environments over the seasons to get an understanding of how we can sustain insect populations through urbanization and climate change.

I feel strongly that scientific research should be paired with public outreach, so in addition to my studies, I have been hosting workshops within NYC community gardens to educate those who live in the area on how to identify and support native bees in their city.

Native bees are tremendously important within their natural ecosystems- especially in urban settings. For years, honeybees, a nonnative species, have served as the poster child for the "Save the Bees" movement, and the reality of the situation is that honeybees have been commodified to the point where they are not going anywhere, but native bees are the ones in danger.

Native bees have co-evolved with native plants, developing specialized physical and behavioral structures that allow them to pollinate more efficiently and better support ecosystem health as a whole. Though native bees are of great environmental significance, they are facing major threats to their existence, and it is not just them. It is projected that we could push 40% of the world's insect species to extinction in the upcoming decades. Insects serve as a key pillar of structural support for ecosystems, and their decline will have cascading effects throughout every region.

In a recent survey of a group of scientists from the Intergovernmental Panel on Climate Change, over 60% of the respondents reported feelings of anxiety, grief, and even distress when thinking about global warming.

It is easy to fall into a loop of doom-filled inactivity and depression when thinking about the climate crisis. The daily flashing headlines showing countless disasters and unforgiving statistics of climbing global temperatures can be discouraging. However, it is important to remember that it is *designed* that way. We are being overwhelmed into a static state to keep us hopeless and passive. It may feel as though we must completely alter our lives to make a difference, but really, simply practicing mindset changes can be extremely impactful.

For example, recycling is not going to solve the climate crisis, and your personal daily work commute is not appreciably responsible for the excess of carbon in the atmosphere. These ideas are part of an intentional strategy to make the individual feel responsible for and in control of expansive pollution committed by multi-billion-dollar companies. It is important to recognize this so that we can advocate for better environmental stewardship on a larger scale as opposed to placing the blame on each other. The mindset associated with tracking the carbon footprint of your neighbor is contributing to our lack of progress. Rather, I suggest that we practice environmental awareness by interacting with nature on smaller scales. This could take the form of gardening, digging your hands into the dirt to create a physical connection with the earth. It is a simple, grounding activity, but the effects on the mind are cosmic.

The most fundamental action we can take in the face of the climate crisis is to invest in our relationship with the natural world. I invite you to take up the idea that choosing native plants in your front yard is a radical act of resistance. I am encouraging you to learn the names of the insect species that live in your garden. By practicing genuine appreciation for your environment, not rooted in methods of control and corporate efficiency but rather a meaningful connection to our world, we can escape the systemic deficiencies that keep us trapped in a destructive cycle.

People who are more in touch with their local environments are the first to speak up against damaging corporate and governmental plans. These include people across the political spectrum united by a genuine understanding and love of their intimately understood environment. When people think of climate protests, what they might not be aware of is that hunters, fishermen, and outdoor enthusiasts of all kinds also share the same main goals, and public awareness through interaction with the environment is a common thread.

We must come to terms with the idea that we can comfortably exist in the same realm as the natural world, and it is not here to serve or benefit us. Once we acknowledge our place, the mundane will become sacred; the everyday will have a greater value than before.

We are facing an onslaught of environmental crises that, if not addressed, will cause irreversible damage to all living things. We could also benefit from observing the mutualistic relationships in nature itself to develop our own interdependent connection to close the perceived gap between nature and humans.

One can simply look to mycelium, a fungus with a web-like structure that develops a mycorrhizal network, allowing plants to give and receive messages warning of danger or disease, as well as transfer nutrients and minerals. If we can mirror the wood wide web and create an above-ground version of mycorrhizal fungi, we can reinvest in our own symbiotic relationships with the natural world as part of a collective effort.

It is essential that we examine the root cause of our environmental plight by learning about anthropocentrism, the belief or philosophy that humans are the most important entities in the universe, from negative mindsets acquired through history and culture, understanding how the human superiority complex is found in our current systems, and accepting that we must work with, not against, the natural world.

The human perception of our disconnectedness from nature can be likened to a "widening gyre," a reverse whirlpool where we find ourselves further from the center, yet we are still forever turning together with the earth as the currents continue to circulate.

By feeling the currents of nature, we can chart a new course together with our world. So, we are in essence all ten years old and lost in the desert.

The situation we find ourselves in is unlike any other we have experienced in our lifetimes, and we have created a hot, dangerous environment, which will be devoid of food and water. In spite of the overwhelming fear, absence of knowledge, and what the road ahead looks like, the only way out is to work together and let the strong will of the youth guide us along the path. Here are several different things you can do right now to be part of the change:

- Plant native plants where you can!
    - If you have a lawn or garden of any kind, be sure to add plants native to your area! This will attract native pollinators, which will be great for the health of your plants and the ecosystem as a whole! Also, native plants often require less maintenance and water than traditional ornamentals because they are adapted to thrive in their home environment!
- Refrain from using fertilizers and pesticides.
    - Fertilizer runoff pollutes nearby waterways, with the excess nitrogen and phosphorus causing harmful algae blooms, which disrupt aquatic plants and animals.
    - Pesticides are often ineffective and contain carcinogenic chemicals that are dangerous to human and environmental health.

- Nature journal.
  - Ecological awareness involves embracing creativity and interconnectedness, which can be achieved through taking time to document observations

Sources:

Francisco Sánchez-Bayo, Kris A.G. Wyckhuys, Worldwide decline of the entomofauna: A review of its drivers, Biological Conservation, Volume 232, 2019, Pages 8-27, ISSN 0006-3207 (https://www.sciencedirect.com/science/article/pii/S0006 320718313636)

Calabria, L., & Marks, E. A scoping review of the impact of eco-distress and coping with distress on the mental health experiences of climate scientists. *Frontiers in psychology*, *15*, 2024, ISSN 1351428. https://doi.org/10.3389/fpsyg.2024.1351428

Yeats, William Butler. "The Second Coming" (1919)

Simard, S., Perry, D., Jones, M. *et al.* Net transfer of carbon between ectomycorrhizal tree species in the field. *Nature* 388, 579–582 (1997). https://doi.org/10.1038/41557

LIVE IT!

Embrace the *moment*

We are all everyday changemakers – each of us contains the ability to make an impact in our own way.

What inspired Katie to be a changemaker?

AUTHOR'S REPLY:

With so many looming environmental dangers on the horizon, I feel that there can be no greater cause to serve than helping find solutions that will address the issues we currently face and provide a more sustainable model for the future.

NOW IT IS YOUR TURN...

What inspires you to be a changemaker?

Katie invites you to reflect with two additional questions:

How does your worldview affect your perspective on nature?

Through what avenues will you practice ecological awareness?

Visit the "Meet the Changemakers" section at the back of the book to connect with and learn more about all of the authors featured in **LIVE IT!**

CHAPTER 10

Inner Best Friend:
How the Most Unexpected Path Leads Us Exactly Where We

Belong

CHANGEMAKER: SARAH JAKLE, MSW, MPP

To my husband Sean, who walked with me
through every step of the journey. I love you.

"However your dream translates through your radiant self is exactly how it was meant to manifest."

– SARAH JAKLE, MSW, MPP

I work with high school girls who often ask me what they should major in for college, with a desperation that in this single choice might lie an entire destiny. I usually smile and tell them life has so many twists and turns that while it feels like a major determines a life, you never know what's ahead. And then I tell them my story.

I started working with the unhoused community with mental illness, getting a master's in social work and a master's in public policy to champion that population. And I thought that would be my career.

Until...

In 2013, I was in a car accident, which left me bedridden with crippling headaches for a year, and just as I was recovering, I was diagnosed with psoriatic arthritis, which bombarded me with horrifying levels of pain and fatigue and disabled my hands. Things got so bad that my rheumatologist put me on disability and gently let me know that I would likely never work again. And I lived for two years with my puppy dog, Max, on a couch. It seemed like the end of my story.

But I'm stubborn. I was also fascinated by what was going on in my own brain. I had been exposed to PTSD research while studying military social work at the University of Southern California, and I started reading about the brain in adverse situations and taking online courses, thinking at the time it was just to grow my internal knowledge and help me respond to this catastrophic turn of events with as much resilience and grace as I could. I knew trauma impacted the amygdala and what we call the limbic system, and I immersed myself in learning the different languages that actually talked to her.

What do I mean when I say different languages? Well, have you ever said to yourself, "Just stop worrying, it's not helpful!" And did that ever work? Never! You're using a rational language to talk to a much older unconscious system—that's our friend, the limbic system.

Some quick brain science: So, in the front of our brain is the prefrontal cortex—this is where we have our rational, conscious thought, and sometimes we think it's the whole brain. But toward the back is the older, faster amygdala, which evolved in caveperson days to unconsciously, constantly scan for threats—part of a larger system called the limbic system. She has a completely different language. And I was fascinated by this limbic system.

I immersed myself in the self-compassion research and practices of Dr. Kristin Neff and the work of Acceptance and Commitment Therapy with Dr. Russ Harris, the work of Dr. Bessel van der Kolk, and so many authors who have thought profoundly about how our body interprets threats and how to facilitate healing. I not only read about trauma, the brain, and the research, but I also practiced mindfulness and self-compassion work and Acceptance and Commitment Therapy meditations. I learned to show up to incredible pain and fatigue with fledgling compassion. To wrap dysregulation and despair with love. And discovering that responding with compassion is actually far more effective than that inner critic who thinks she's so helpful. It doesn't "fix"—it opens room around difficulty to respond differently.

Then the election of 2016 happened. And I thought, "I cannot sit this out on the couch. I need to get up." But I also noticed that every time I had the intention to get up, my brain would overwhelm me with pain and fatigue and wave off taking action. So, I started to specifically apply all the skills I'd been learning:

- From the compassion work of Dr. Neff, I internalized what I started to call "inner best friend" figures: my sweet puppy, Max, and Barack Obama, who encouraged and supported me.
- I noticed when I was getting flooded with anxiety and would invoke the skill called "grounding," which asks the brain to notice being in firm contact with the floor, because the act of asking the brain to notice pulls you from the anxious limbic system into the more rational prefrontal cortex.
- Every night with my husband, we would go through things we were grateful for during the day, because gratitude helps the brain shift from its negativity bias to being more open to noticing positive things and gently re-orient us to see possibilities.
- When I wanted to register voters but was overwhelmed before I started, I broke it down. I said to myself, "Just get in the car, sweet pea." "Just drive there, sweet pea, you can drive home if you need to." "Just register one voter, sweet pea."

And I repeated this over and over so successfully that after the 2018 midterms, I became the National Outreach Director of a new voter registration group called Field Team 6 and then, beyond my wildest expectations, the Get Out The Vote Director for The California National Organization for Women.

It was here I saw something fascinating: even though women are amazing leaders, we are not nearly equally represented in the electoral space. In 2025, women made up only 28% of Congress, and only 9% of Congress were women of color, even though women make up 51% of the population and women of color make up 20% of the population. The other thing I saw was that when women did step up, they received much more pushback than their male counterparts - which was amplified in the electoral space but again is true in every industry. On Facebook in 2020, Republican women got twice as much harassment as Republican men, and Democratic women got ten *times* as much harassment as Democratic men. I heard from many women who didn't want to run because of the amount of hate that we basically accept as part of a woman's elected leadership journey.

And I started wondering what the impact of all of this would be on the brain. Because, remember, I'd been studying and looking at the brain and the unconscious anxious limbic system now for many years. And being screamed at dysregulates the limbic system. Being dismissed dysregulates the limbic system. Certainly, rape threats or being called a "bitch" dysregulate the limbic system. I knew there were evidence-based practices to help.

People have spent decades researching how to help dysregulated limbic systems. We just haven't typically brought that knowledge to how we train women civic leaders. Normally, like me, women will acquire the skills to help regulate their limbic systems later in life because of suffering or burnout. But what if we just gave the skills to young women? What if high school girls were trained in skills to help regulate limbic systems so they could start sprinting ahead, protected? As I looked into it, high school was the last time boys and girls thought they could run for office equally. It's the perfect time to give them the right skills to stay on their critical civic and elected leadership paths rather than restarting them after they stall.

What if we gave high school girls the public policy training to immediately be confident, effective, informed advocates in their own communities, and also instill in them that running for office is their birthright?

And what if we backed up each one of the public policy skills with a specific evidence-based practice psychology skill to help them shift their self-talk, normalize, name, and overcome impostor syndrome, and regulate their limbic systems when they were either filled with

self-doubt or receiving real pushback in a space? What if we not only set women up to be confident civic leaders, but also included the skills to successfully cope with the forces that try to push them off their leadership journey? Both internalized narratives that derail amazing women and also the external forces consciously trying to drown out their voices and extinguish their light?

My organization, DemocraShe, was born—a nonpartisan nonprofit offering national, online, peer-led training in public policy skills matched with evidence-based resiliency skills to protect their limbic systems from the pushback we know women receive—amplified across any intersectional identity. Pipelines of high school girls around the country set up with a full toolbox to make their brains their allies and step confidently into immediate civic advocacy in our democracy and be our earliest bench of future elected leaders. And since our founding in January 2021, we have, as of this writing, served 1500 girls in forty-one states.

This is what I tell the young women I work with: sometimes only in retrospect can we see that a very windy journey came together for a single purpose: if I hadn't gone through extreme suffering, both mental and physical, I wouldn't have sought out the training to shift my own self-talk and regulate my own trauma and distress. If I hadn't been passionate about helping people with suffering, I wouldn't have sought out two master's degrees that now came together in a Venn diagram for how to move young women forward.

If I hadn't learned both through studying and my own experience that not only is compassion a lovely way to be, but it's actually much more effective and motivating us to reach our goals than the harsh internal bully we think is helping, I wouldn't be able to shower vibrant, extraordinary high school girls with a space of unconditional love and support where our motto is "you can't do it wrong" and watch them blossom as we teach them to internalize that love and compassion for themselves and gently encourage themselves to step out of their comfort zones and trust their voice and worth—and skills—when they receive pushback.

That sometimes, only through retrospect, do we see we arrived at exactly where we belonged. That only in absolute desperation, finding my own "inner best friend" did that emerge as a skill I can instill in young women to support them, encourage them, and love them as they do hard but valuable things as civic and elected leaders.

I still encounter things that seem to derail my path. I give myself the space to grieve hardships and losses, to eschew "toxic positivity" that denies humans the space to feel supported in their full emotions. I also know that sometimes in the moments that seem to take me most off my initial path can lie the seeds of a path I never knew I most wanted.

LIVE IT!

Embrace the *moment*

We are all everyday changemakers – each of us contains the ability to make an impact in our own way.

What inspires Sarah to be a changemaker?

AUTHOR'S REPLY:

Helping women understand they are amazing! AND there are evidence-based social work skills to help with the difficult parts of life we all face—no one does this alone. Women deserve not only to lead in every space but also to thrive.

NOW IT IS YOUR TURN...

What inspires you to be a changemaker?

Sarah invites you to reflect with two additional questions:

When life reroutes you through pain, fatigue, or loss, what tools can you lean on right now to keep moving forward, even if it's just one small "sweet pea" step?

How will you let your prefrontal cortex take the wheel and not allow your amygdala to keep you stuck in fear? Which part of your brain will you choose to lead you today?

Visit the "Meet the Changemakers" section at the back of the book to connect with and learn more about all of the authors featured in **LIVE IT!**

CHAPTER 11

Live

a Good Story

CHANGEMAKER: TARA MARIE STEMKOVSKY

To my heroes — my children, Cole and Sonya.

May you always have the courage to speak your truth,
and the strength to turn your pain into purpose.

"Let the pain that once silenced you —
fuel your voice — and change the world."

– TARA MARIE STEMKOVSKY

*M*y nickname as a child was "Tara the Terror." It was given to me by loving family members. If something *could* be destroyed, I'd find a way. Snipping the strings off Grandma's new blinds? Sure! Testing a can of pink paint on the new gray carpet? Absolutely! Looking back, I realize I wasn't trying to cause trouble. I was brimming with curiosity, creativity, and a deep need to understand how the world worked—and to get others to understand it, too.

Then, one October morning, my world cracked wide open.

I was nine when my mother woke my sister and me and told us to come downstairs. Our godfather, Don—my dad's best friend and a fellow detective—was there. His wife, Ellen, suddenly walked out of the room in tears. My mom turned to us and said, *"The FBI thinks your father is a bank robber."*

I thought I'd misheard. My father was a decorated detective; he couldn't possibly be a criminal. It's remarkable how the mind holds onto trauma's details like a film to replay over time. Decades later, I still remember the lighting, where I sat on the couch, and how I couldn't look at my mother because her eyes were red from crying.

Soon, the media frenzy began. Newscasters painted our lives in wealth and greed—Cadillacs in the driveway and golden faucets in the home. Most of it lies. In 1991, there was no social media, no platform to control and set the record straight. Once the media told your story, it stuck.

My mother lost her entire support system overnight. Despite my father's seventeen years on the force, the officers and wives we once called family turned their backs the moment the FBI came knocking. His pension—forfeited. And prisoners don't pay child support. Stunned, my mother had no choice but to enter the workforce as a single mother.

At school, my sister and I were ostracized. Many parents told their children not to associate with us. Rumors followed me through the hallways and onto the school bus. The shame was constant.

Eventually, my father pleaded guilty. He said he'd been hearing voices and experiencing hallucinations—symptoms consistent with a prison psychologist's diagnosis of manic depression and psychosis. During his bail hearing, I learned for the first time that my father had endured horrific childhood abuse by his uncle and stepfather, relentless instability, and over fourteen school changes. Still, he was denied bail and sentenced to thirteen years in federal prison.

My mother turned down offers from talk shows like Phil Donahue and Geraldo Rivera. Only recently did she explain to me her reasoning: silence was the only way she knew how to protect her children since the media had already vilified us. She wanted the story to go away so everyone would forget. Unfortunately, her silence was misinterpreted by many as guilt.

Films became my escape. In *those* stories, even villains had nuanced backstories that invited empathy. I became obsessed with the power of storytelling: how a camera, a script, music, and a vision could transport audiences and ignite compassion. As a pre-teen, I began borrowing my dad's old video camera to make silly home movies.

At 14, I stumbled across an HBO documentary: *Paradise Lost: The Child Murders at Robin Hood Hills*. It followed the West Memphis Three—teenagers accused of killing three young boys in Arkansas. The filmmakers convinced HBO to document the entire trial, which was rare at the time. As I watched, I became convinced of their innocence. For the first time, I saw that film could do more than entertain—it could expose injustice. And I was completely captivated.

By college, I knew I loved film, but I worried *others* would see it as impractical. Instead, I chose broadcast journalism as my major and film theory as a minor. I told myself I'd learn to shoot and write for news—and maybe, just maybe, find my way into deeper storytelling later.

In college, I created a presentation on the flaws of capital punishment. Afterward, my professor said I had the presence for network anchoring. But that never felt right to me. Reading a teleprompter lacked soul. Plus, the idea of going live terrified me. I was constantly afraid of messing up on air and being judged for it—once again, a target of public scrutiny.

After graduation, I struggled to break into the media. I waitressed, managed restaurants, and eventually landed a temp job at a major nonprofit. It wasn't the fast-paced media job I'd dreamed of, but it paid the bills and surrounded me with supportive people. Still, I craved a creative outlet—something that reconnected me to emotional storytelling.

Since no one was offering me the job I wanted, I gave myself one: I started a wedding videography business. It wasn't glamorous, but it let me tell emotional, meaningful stories on my own terms.

Then, in 2011, I found myself back in the orbit of the West Memphis Three. After decades of advocacy, the case made international headlines—much of it propelled by the HBO documentaries that exposed the case's deep flaws. Public outrage had reached a fever pitch. In a stunning turn of events, the three men were summoned to court and offered an Alford plea deal—a rare legal arrangement allowing them to assert their innocence while conceding that the state had enough evidence to convict them. In exchange, they were released with credit for time served: more than eighteen years behind bars. For me, their release was a historic moment—a powerful intersection of justice and storytelling. It was proof that film could be more than a tool for awareness; it could be a catalyst for impossible change. I wanted to be part of something that was meaningful. I just didn't know how to start.

Around that same time, I met and later married a jazz critic, who was also an insightful, talented musician. After a long struggle with infertility, we finally welcomed two children. For a while, it felt like I'd found peace.

But gradually, cracks formed.

My husband's perfectionism, once a strength in his professional world, clashed with the beautiful chaos of raising children. The sharp critiques he once directed toward jazz compositions began to turn toward me and the children. Name-calling escalated. His impossible expectations created a tense, toxic undercurrent in our home.

I tried to ignore it. I told myself that I'd survived worse. I wore headphones to drown it out. *What's some yelling? At least he's not hitting me.*

But then one day, I looked at my kids—and realized *they* hadn't been desensitized the way I had. They were absorbing everything. I refused to let them grow up that way. I gave my husband an ultimatum: stop the behavior in front of the children or leave.

We tried counseling. In one of my solo sessions, my therapist carefully explained, *"'Ab-normal' means away from normal. It's the same with 'ab-use'—it's an abnormal use of something. Tara, you're in an abusive relationship."*

And there it was—I was in an emotionally abusive marriage. I hadn't even known that was a thing. I just thought he was demanding. I didn't realize that name-calling could be abuse.

My therapist helped me realize I had been shrinking myself my entire life—trying to prove I wasn't like my father, that I wasn't an erratic troublemaker. After growing up under the weight of public criticism, I carried a deeply rooted fear of judgment. I constantly assumed people were talking about me—angrily behind my back. The gaslighting in my marriage just confirmed the message I'd internalized long ago: *no one would ever believe your side anyway.*

Our marriage counselor eventually said the words I had been too afraid to admit out loud: the marriage was beyond repair, and it was time to discuss divorce.

And just like that, the dream I'd clung to—the happy, stable home I wanted for my children—evaporated.

What followed was nothing short of survival. The grief and exhaustion crushed me. I stopped filming. Entire years disappeared into a fog.

But my children—my heroes—wouldn't let me disappear this time. The instinct to protect and care for them overpowered any pain I was carrying. In showing up for them, I kept myself from unraveling. Eventually, I picked up my camera again—not for clients, but to document their laughter, their growth, and our fleeting moments together.

As I healed, I began sharing my experience with emotional abuse. I didn't expect a response. But slowly, messages trickled in. Some were strangers. Some were friends. They thanked me. They said my words helped them recognize the abuse in their own lives.

For the first time, my voice had power. And I was ready to use it.

Then, in 2021, the Gabby Petito case exploded in the news. Gabby, a twenty-two-year-old travel vlogger, went missing on a cross-country trip with her fiancé. He returned home alone, but Gabby was later found dead. He died by suicide, leaving behind a confession.

What haunted me wasn't just the tragedy—it was the police bodycam footage recorded days prior to her disappearance. Gabby was clearly distressed, yet police labeled her the aggressor. They missed every red flag. The signs were obvious to anyone who understood abuse dynamics. But every officer on site missed the clues.

I was furious. Furious for Gabby—and for every woman like her. And I realized I *could* do something. I had my voice, my camera, and a decade of experience. I didn't need a network or permission: I started a YouTube channel.

My very first video—a deep dive into a separate, highly controversial high-profile case—took off instantly. Thousands of views poured in, and at first, I was thrilled.

But then came the comments. Hundreds of them. Many weren't about the case—they were about *me*. *My* intelligence. *My* worth.

I stopped creating for months. The fear of being ridiculed came roaring back. I had finally dared to use my voice more publicly with my passion, and I felt like the world just confirmed every reason I'd stayed silent for so long.

But then, a message arrived from a viewer:

"Thank you for discussing this case in a different way than the mass media has for decades. Don't let the lynch mob get to you. Many people believe this is a wrongful

conviction, rooted in prosecutorial and police misconduct. Thank you for your fair and honest storytelling."

That simple message empowered me. I realized: real people who didn't have the ability—or safety—to speak needed help. People whose stories had been buried, still waiting for justice. Then I realized, strangely, my past had prepared me. I was already resilient to public shaming, and now the hate fueled the algorithm and engagement—amplifying the stories I told. The people trying to tear me down were, without knowing it, helping the cause.

That shift in perspective changed everything.

Today, my content has reached millions. I work with families still searching for justice. And that first case I covered—the one that drew so much hate? It's now being reviewed by a chapter of The Innocence Project. They believe they can prove factual innocence—and that police destroyed key exonerating evidence.

In my home, there's a hand-drawn phrase framed in the entryway: *Live a good story.*

To me, that doesn't mean a perfect life. It means embracing your whole truth—the pain, the joy, the survival. It means rising from what nearly broke you and not being afraid to share it. Because your story has power. It can connect us. To influence laws. To spark change. And the thing that once felt like your weakness? It might just be your hidden superpower.

So I ask you: *what was the most painful chapter in your life? And what might happen if you finally chose to share it?*

If you're still holding back—because of fear, shame, or the weight of other people's opinions—remember this: You hold the pen. Be bold enough to tell your story—and brave enough to live a good one.

LIVE IT!
Embrace the *moment*

We are all everyday changemakers – each of us contains the ability to make an impact in our own way.

What inspired Tara to be a changemaker?

AUTHOR'S REPLY:
Helping others understand the red flags of addiction, mental illness, and abuse while using my platform to help seek justice for the innocent.

NOW IT IS YOUR TURN...

What inspires you to be a changemaker?

Tara invites you to reflect with two additional questions:

What survival patterns am I still carrying, and are they helping or harming me today?

What truth have I been afraid to say out loud, and what would change if I finally said it?

Visit the "Meet the Changemakers" section at the back of the book to connect with and learn more about all of the authors featured in **LIVE IT!**

CHAPTER 12

How Did We Get Here?

CHANGEMAKER: JANET KOTSAKIS

To my husband, Chris and my son, Dean.

Thank you for letting me be me.

Whatever I do, I do for you.

" When I find myself handling something that once
would've overwhelmed me, I pause and remember:
this ease was earned. Somewhere in my past—
through a job I didn't enjoy, a tough relationship, or
a season of chaos—God was quietly preparing me.
Every challenge was training for this very moment."

– JANET KOTSAKIS

"How did we get here?!" It's a question often asked in frustration. But on a crisp April morning in 2025, it was asked with joy. Over eggs and bacon at a Jersey diner, the executive team of the Food Bank of South Jersey (FBSJ) marked six transformative years together. We were celebrating the leadership team assembled by CEO Fred Wasiak: Chief Operating Officer Charlie Hosier, Chief Development Officer Lavinia Awosanya, me (Chief People Officer Janet Kotsakis), and the final piece of our puzzle, Chief Financial Officer Kathleen Horton. When she walked into our Pennsauken office in 2019, none of us knew just how close-knit and impactful this team would become. Together, along with the staff, we would go on to Raise the B.A.R.—Belonging, Achievement, Relationships—for our organization and become Better Together.

We began our journey just a year before the COVID-19 pandemic brought the world to a halt and hurtled our food bank into a new level of service to the food-insecure children, seniors, and families across Burlington, Camden, Gloucester, and Salem Counties. In 2019, FBSJ had forty-three employees and distributed 10.4 million pounds of food. By 2020, we had grown to sixty-four staff members and distributed 22.5 million pounds. That number would grow to 23.4 million pounds in 2024, supported by a staff of ninety-eight. The need exploded—and it never subsided.

During the pandemic, food banks became national symbols of resilience and support. Lines of cars stretched for miles, waiting for assistance. People saw what we did—and never forgot. That recognition has turned into sustained demand for our services.

The pandemic was a test of our fortitude and leadership. However, the groundwork we laid in the year leading up to it gave us the resilience to meet the moment. That foundation was built on trust, courage, and a belief in our people.

A New Beginning: Fred's First Day

That foundation started on November 5, 2018—Fred Wasiak's first day at FBSJ. At the time, the organization was struggling with morale. Raises had not been given in recent years. Ideas weren't solicited, let alone welcomed. Trust was at a low point.

Fred reached out before his official start date and requested a full staff meeting on his first day. But his first staff meeting wasn't a speech. It was a workshop. Fred began by introducing "Raising the B.A.R."—a framework centered on Belonging, Achievement, and Relationships. The idea was that if an organization promotes Relationships and cultivates a culture of Belonging, it can Achieve great things. He split employees into six "Neighborhoods," each tasked with answering two questions: "What are you most proud of?" and "What can we do better?" Then, each group chose one actionable idea to improve the workplace. The results: initiatives focused on culture, communication, interdepartmental process improvement, safety, LEAN methodology, and cross-training.

At that time, Lavinia was Director of Fund Development, Charlie was Director of Operations, and I was Executive

Assistant. Although Charlie knew Fred from a past community service experience, we did not know if this guy was "for real" (to put it nicely). What in the world did these projects have to do with repairing our organization? Between these neighborhoods and his passion for Mindful Leadership and Emotional Intelligence, we weren't sure if this guy was a little goofy, though he seemed nice enough.

While the neighborhoods tackled their SMART goals, Fred quietly started building his team. Charlie became COO. Lavinia was promoted to CDO in spring 2019. Fred sat me down and said he was bringing on a full-time HR leader—and he wanted that person to be me. I said a firm, "No, thank you." I was not interested in the responsibility of HR, didn't want to fire people, and, by the way, I had no experience or training in that field. Fred didn't flinch. He eagerly responded that I had more relevant experience than I realized; the organization needed this position; the staff trusted me, and I was the right person for the job. It is difficult to resist that kind of persuasion. Having someone tell you that they see something in you and believe that you can be more than you ever thought possible is a powerful thing. It would not be the last time Fred used his persuasive powers to earn his nickname, "The Gentle Disruptor." I said yes. Kathleen joined in April 2019, completing our team.

The Team Assembles!

Our executive team had reached the first step in Psychologist Bruce Tuckman's group development model—Forming. We didn't all know each other yet, and we were a little wary. The former administration was known for setting goals that put departments in conflict with one another, and I think a lot of that friction and distrust were still present. But one thing we all shared was a passion for feeding people in need in South Jersey and a deep appreciation and respect for our employees. We continue to believe in doing the right thing for them, always.

Our diversity of experience and expertise proved to be our strength. Fred brought an energizing mix of YMCA leadership and consulting experience, rooted in emotional intelligence. Charlie, with his warehouse and manufacturing background, provided operational expertise. Lavinia knew and understood our donors and fundraising, eventually earning both a CFRE and an MBA. Kathleen, a seasoned finance executive and former business owner, brought a mix of business acumen and compliance knowledge. I knew the staff—our concerns, history, and hopes—and eventually earned a SHRM-CP. I felt – and continue to feel – fully supported. I had the freedom to make mistakes and learn from each of them, which is a tremendous gift.

The interesting thing about Tuckman's model is that the steps don't always follow the exact order of Forming, Storming, Norming, and Performing, and that was true of our group. In addition to these phases happening in our executive team, it was happening for the whole organization as well. I remember having a meeting with the Culture Club neighborhood, where I began to talk about the need for improving morale and creating a new culture. Someone looked at me skeptically and said, "I know

NOTHING about creating culture. That's YOUR job as an HR person, and Fred's job as CEO." They weren't wrong, historically. We had come from a place where our culture was handed down to us. Things were not typically discussed as a group; they were dictated to us. I explained—based on many conversations I'd already had with Fred and the executive team—that our staff members had a voice and could contribute to our organization. Culture was "the way we do things" and was up to the staff to determine now, and we would learn how to do that together.

Trust and Tangible Change

It was clear from the start that changing the culture would be one of the key elements that would allow us to move forward. We also knew that building trust was the way to make that happen. Remember those neighborhoods? They were a great way to allay the Storming experienced by our team at this point. Our executive team's work included encouraging feedback and building trust by honoring commitments. We set about adjusting equity in compensation, promotions, and training. Culture only goes so far if not supported by fair practices.

In the meantime, those SMART goals the neighborhoods had set were beginning to bear fruit. "The Food Bank Buzz" newsletter was started, and we hung monitors throughout the organization to facilitate better communication. We brought in local experts who taught staff how to be more efficient, using LEAN concepts. We started Learning

Through Service, allowing employees to experience other departments by spending time shadowing each year. Perhaps most importantly, our Culture Club received training on how to develop company values, and at a staff meeting, facilitated the creation of our current Values— Collaboration, Integrity, Inclusion, Service, Dedication, and Versatility. We continue to incorporate those Values into our everyday activities and annual planning. They contributed to our ability to "Norm" as an organization. Everyone now knew what the expectations were.

Our executive team remains supportive of each other to this day, but that doesn't mean we don't Storm occasionally. Imagine trying to turn the organization around with a seemingly radical new culture—encouraging every voice to be heard. An example of one of the "storms" we experienced was making sure everyone on the staff had the time and opportunity to participate in the neighborhood work and make their best contribution. Having Order Pullers and other hourly workers leave their posts to attend a meeting every few weeks or to attend training was a new concept for some of our leaders. It caused problems with other staff and with supervisors. But we listened. And we invested—not just in budgets for training or overtime—but in mentorship, shadowing, and growth opportunities. We showed people we believed in them and were willing to back it up. Slowly, it changed everything.

Building a Resilient Organization

With the help of our neighborhoods, culture was improving. The leadership team, including the directors, were now focusing on structure and sustainability. We evaluated our org chart to ensure people were in the right roles. We introduced a clear compensation philosophy that included meaningful annual assessments that allowed us to reward work well done. We assessed our technology, logistics, and planning capacity.

In 2020, these improvements would become our Strategic Plan—Fred called it "20/20 Vision" (he loves a good dad joke). One key initiative was replacing desktop computers with laptops. A seemingly small change, but when the pandemic hit, it meant our team members could pivot fast by working from home when possible and keep serving those in need.

All these steps—from new technology to new culture—helped us to reach Tuckman's fourth step in his model – Performing. It allowed us not only to survive the pandemic but to lead through it.

In the chaos of 2020, the neighborhood format was not sustainable in its original form. However, much of the work started by those original groups continues, and the desire for us to do our best work by Raising the B.A.R. became a part of the organization's DNA.

Reflecting on the Journey

Over one last cup of coffee in that diner last April, we took some time to reflect together on the questions, "How did we get here?" and "What makes us so different?" How had we not only lasted six years together, but done it through a global crisis and with genuine camaraderie?

Kathleen spoke first, "For me, it's trust. Each team member has the best interests of the Food Bank of South Jersey at heart every time they make a decision. Also, Fred, your humility and openness to hear our concerns and change your mind (as appropriate) is a special quality in a CEO."

As each team member spoke, it became apparent that trust was the common denominator for each of us, as well as a belief that we succeed by putting the organization first.

Charlie added, "I know I sleep well at night knowing that while our decisions may not always be popular, they are made to help our team. We are willing to talk things through and explain our rationales for the decisions that we make. Eventually, we can agree and walk in the same direction."

Fred nodded. "Solid relationships are built on trust. Trial and error. Open minds. Being present, listening to others. Our experiences complement each other well. I'm a better person because I have served alongside all of you."

We often joke, "No one grows up saying, 'I want to be a food banker.'" But we all believe that everything in our past prepared us for being here in this place, at the crucial moment when it was essential for us to be at our best for our organization and the people we serve. When needed, we were able to show up—Better Together.

LIVE IT!

Embrace the *moment*

We are all everyday changemakers – each of us contains the ability to make an impact in our own way.

What inspired Janet to be a changemaker?

AUTHOR'S REPLY:
My faith. To be a good example for my son. The people I am lucky enough to work with everyday.

NOW IT IS YOUR TURN...

What inspires you to be a changemaker?

Janet invites you to reflect with two additional questions:

What does Belonging mean to you, and why is it important?

What could change if you said "Yes" more often? Even when it was scary?

Visit the "Meet the Changemakers" section at the back of the book to connect with and learn more about all of the authors featured in **LIVE IT!**

LIVE IT! *reflection*

Do What is Right: A Message of Karma and Dharma

"It's not always easy to do what's right, but with time, I've learned it's always worth it."

– MOHAN METLA

I pass on the advice I learned from my own father to my kids. I always tell them this gem of advice, and I'll say it again at every chance: do what is right. Not just because it sounds good, but because it is the essence of karma and dharma. These are not just words in Sanskrit, the ancient language of my native India; they are the primary principles that have shaped my life from a young age and have gotten me through the challenges of life. My father once sat down with me and explained karma and dharma. It became part of my education before high school, we studied Sanskrit, not as a luxury, but as a foundation for life.

Karma to us is action. Dharma is also duty. When you live with both principles, I tell my kids, your life reflects integrity. In their school and academics, in their afterschool sports, I remind them, no matter the temptation to cut corners, to choose the correct path. That is what defines their future legacy.

In my career journey, I have been entrusted with handling challenges—but also with providing solutions. I sometimes start my sentences with "the challenge is," but then I recall I am not just there to point out what's wrong; I am there to bring solutions. To think differently. To plan ahead. And to solve the challenge. Not just with skill, but with character. And nine out of ten times, those I helped solve problems have come back to me again because they trust me.

Know that your integrity is never outdated. Carry your expertise and skills with humility. When you walk the path of karma and dharma, you are not only doing what is right—you are lighting the path for others to follow.

Mohan invites you to reflect on these two questions:

What is one key insight or lesson from this chapter that you can apply to your own life, and how might it influence your future decisions or actions?

What values or lessons from your own upbringing continue to guide your decisions today, and how do you live by those principles?

Visit the "Meet the Changemakers" section at the back of the book to connect with and learn more about all of the authors featured in **LIVE IT!**

CHAPTER 13

SHE IS HOPE LA:
From Suitcase to
Success

CHANGEMAKER: TISHA JANIGIAN

To my sons, Nicholas and Alexander Momjian,
and my parents, Nelson and Nancy Janigian.

"Together, we make a greater impact."

– TISHA JANIGIAN

$\mathcal{M}$y journey from personal hardship to becoming a transformative leader and advocate for single mothers is a testament to the power of resilience, determination, and a deep desire to uplift others. As a mother of two young men, my life took a dramatic turn after my divorce in 2012, with just a suitcase each—no money, no credit, and no assets. Despite these challenges, I refused to be defined by my circumstances and instead channeled my struggle into building a legacy of hope for other single mothers.

I was raised by parents who taught me the value of giving back. My parents led by example—selfless, hardworking, and generous even when times were tough. Their compassion and entrepreneurship shaped me. Experiencing struggle firsthand fueled my belief that no one should have to face the same pain alone—and that belief has shaped my life's work.

When I moved back to Los Angeles to give my sons a better future, one person took a chance on me, allowing my father to co-sign for an apartment. That hand up—not a handout—is exactly what SHE IS HOPE LA now strives to provide for other single mothers: a new purpose, a new direction, and a new hope, just as someone once did for me.

Those early days were filled with uncertainty. Many nights I lay awake, wondering how I'd get through the next day or whether I'd be able to keep a roof over our heads. But looking at my sons, I knew I could not give up. I wanted to show them that no matter how hard life gets, you keep moving forward. They became my driving force, giving me the strength to push through even the hardest days and prove that with hard work, anything is possible.

In 2012, I searched for full-time work but couldn't afford childcare—my parents were in another state, unable to sell their home and follow me back. Part-time jobs became my only option, but many employers told me I was overqualified because of my bachelor's degree. When I did secure part-time work, my food stamp benefits dropped to nearly nothing. I realized that staying home would have brought in more support but wouldn't have built a future. So, I took a leap of faith, accepted the job offer, and started sharing my story. That vulnerability opened unexpected doors.

Other parents offered me babysitting and pet-sitting jobs, and I signed up for focus groups to earn small stipends—sometimes even having my children participate when they qualified. We'd split the money because every bit helped, and it taught them the value of working together as a family.

I built connections with other parents to share school pickups and playdates, weaving together a small community of support. I signed up for every discount program imaginable—low-income utility assistance, WIC, food stamps, library programs, even donated plasma—and bought groceries and toys from the dollar stores. On Black Friday, I'd stand in long lines, hoping to find something special for the boys—anything beyond the dollar store toys they were used to. I learned to get creative, rotating toys and storing many away so that when I brought them back out months later, they felt brand new again.

I scoured Freecycle and Craigslist to furnish our apartment and resold what we didn't need to make a little extra money. I visited thrift stores on dollar days to look for household items and clothes we needed, ran yard sales, and took in furniture left behind by neighbors to flip for cash—or to make our apartment feel a little more like home. I also consigned clothing for all of us, which helped stretch our budget and get new items as the boys grew so quickly. Every little effort, every creative solution, was another way to make life just a bit more comfortable for them.

Meals were simple and often repetitive. I'd stir peas into boxed macaroni and cheese just to get a few vegetables into the boys' diets. On many nights, dinner was nothing more than eggs or cereal.

I found free birthday meals online, signed up for Kids Bowl Free during the summer, and took my boys to museums on free admission days. I learned to find joy and adventure in places others might overlook and built memories with very little.

There were days when I had to choose between paying a bill and buying groceries. I stretched every dollar, sold items online, and took every odd job I could find.

I felt so alone.

I'd turn to retail therapy for comfort—only to realize I couldn't afford anything and would return it all the next day. I had no idea then that those very struggles would become the foundation for a nonprofit that would one day help countless women rise above their own challenges.

Six months in, I wasn't making enough money to pay the next month's rent and had nowhere to go. Section 8 housing had years-long waitlists. I felt defeated—until an opportunity arose. A full-time management role opened up at the company where I worked, and I decided to go for it! We needed something to change, and I mustered all my strength for the interview and got the promotion. That was a game-changer for us! At the same time, my folks finally got an offer on their rural property. They sold their home at a loss and moved back to Los Angeles to help us.

Through their help and my new job, we managed to qualify for a house. We stayed there for two years, flipped it, and used the money to buy my parents another home. I moved my boys to an apartment in another school district. Six years later, my parents' house doubled in value, and I was able to use that profit as a down payment for the home we're in now. I'm now able to support my parents, who live with us, and my sons finally have their own rooms—and even better, we also house a single mom and her child as they work toward rebuilding their lives.

Many of the single mothers we serve today are just like I once was—in survival mode, doing whatever it takes to keep food on the table and a roof overhead. I saw firsthand how the system is built to keep people dependent, not to lift them up. This fueled my mission for SHE IS HOPE LA: to bridge that gap and give single mothers the tools, support, and community they need to not just survive, but thrive.

In 2019, I officially launched SHE IS HOPE LA, and shortly after, SHE IS HOPE Realty, to give single mothers that same hand up I once received—and to create a long-term, sustainable funding model for the nonprofit.

It was my father who first encouraged me to get into real estate. After spending most of my life in sales, he saw that I had both the experience and the heart to succeed. Real estate offered the flexibility I needed as a single mom and had the potential for high income—something I knew could not only change my life but help change the lives of others, too. So, I studied, got licensed, and built something meaningful from the ground up.

What differentiates SHE IS HOPE Realty is our mission-driven approach. We donate a portion of every real estate commission directly back to the nonprofit, allowing us to fund vital programs and services for single mothers and their children. Whether we're helping someone find their first home or sell an investment property, we're also helping a single mom find stability, security, and support.

We're a boutique California brokerage of purpose-driven professionals, including my sons—driven by the belief that real estate can be both a business and a force for good. From residential and commercial sales to investment, relocation, and property management, we handle it all with care and purpose. Every transaction helps build stability, strengthen communities, and continue a legacy of hope and impact.

Every single one of our nonprofit programs was born from personal experience. When I had to choose between working and losing benefits, I knew we needed job training programs with flexible schedules. When I couldn't afford childcare, I knew we needed a network to support moms with resources for their kids. When I had to sell furniture and electronics to make rent, I knew a donation center and resale boutique could make a difference. We don't just run programs; we build lifelines—because I've lived it.

And we don't do it alone.

One of the most powerful forces behind our mission at SHE IS HOPE LA is the spirit of collaboration. We're proud to stand alongside incredible nonprofits and mission-aligned partners who serve veterans, domestic violence survivors, displaced families, aged-out foster youth, and those facing housing insecurity. By uniting our resources, referrals, and hearts, we amplify one another's efforts and ensure that no one is ever forgotten or left behind.

Every mother's story fuels my passion and reminds me of my own. For me, each success is not just a personal win, it's a victory for the entire community of single mothers we serve. Every closing through my real estate brokerage helps fund SHE IS HOPE LA's programs; each new initiative breaks the cycle of instability; and every single mother we reach brings us closer to lasting change.

One of the things that makes me most proud is seeing the ripple effect of this work in action. Many of the single mothers who once came to us for support now stand beside me, helping others find their way forward. Some have started their own nonprofits; others have launched businesses, returned to school, earned degrees they once thought were out of reach, and built the stable lives they deserve.

One story that holds a special place in my heart is that of a single mother who came to SHE IS HOPE LA while working multiple jobs to provide for her children. She was exhausted, juggling shift work with no benefits, and constantly worried about how she would manage when one of her children got sick. Through our program, she received career counseling, job training, financial literacy workshops, basic household resources, and—most importantly—a community that had her back.

With time, she was able to go back to school and earn a degree. Today, she works full-time in a field she loves, with benefits that give her peace of mind. She recently launched her own nonprofit—continuing the cycle of support that helped her rise. We still help each other regularly, because that's what SHE IS HOPE LA is all about: lasting relationships, lifelong growth, and building something bigger than ourselves.

Together, we are stronger. We lift one another up and remind each other that we are never alone. Seeing these incredible women give back, volunteer, mentor, and pay it forward proves to me every day that when one mother rises, we all rise.

Looking back, I'm amazed at how far we've come. From barely scraping by to now running a thriving nonprofit and brokerage, this journey has been transformative. My sons have watched me fight for every step forward, and I hope they see now that with hope, determination, and hard work; anything is possible.

I envision a future where SHE IS HOPE LA grows far beyond Los Angeles—reaching across the nation and eventually the world—creating communities where every single mother has the support, tools, and belief she needs to thrive.

It's never too late to begin again, to transform struggle into strength, or to write a story filled with hope and possibility. I've learned that when we lift one another up—the ripple becomes a wave of lasting change.

Together, we make a greater impact.

LIVE IT!

Embrace the *moment*

We are all everyday changemakers – each of us contains the ability to make an impact in our own way.

What inspired Tisha to be a changemaker?

AUTHOR'S REPLY:

I was inspired to become a changemaker to prevent others from experiencing the hardships I faced when I had to start over with nothing. I wanted to show my sons that with resilience, determination, and heart, you can rebuild your life, make your dreams come true, and lift others as you rise.

NOW IT IS YOUR TURN...

What inspires you to be a changemaker?

Tisha invites you to reflect with two additional questions:

When life feels overwhelming, what helps you reconnect with hope and possibility?

How can you use your own skills, resources, or experiences to create a ripple effect of hope in your community?

Visit the "Meet the Changemakers" section at the back of the book to connect with and learn more about all of the authors featured in **LIVE IT!**

CHAPTER 14

How Many Mariah Carey

Moments

Did You Have?

CHANGEMAKER: NICOL NICOLA, DBA

To Kris Lew, who taught me to appreciate
Mariah Carey's music, and made attending her
holiday concert an annual tradition!

"Keep It Simple"

– NICOL NICOLA, DBA

As a young person, I always viewed challenges as monumental hurdles. It took me many years to reframe my thinking and see challenges as windows and a way to "grow through this pain," as one of my favorite singers, Robbie Williams, says in his song, "Better Man." This shift in mindset helped me develop great coping skills. Even now, when I face difficult situations, people, or projects, I remind myself that each challenge could be a coachable moment, a stepping stone toward something better.

There are many examples in my life that highlight how I once defaulted to a victim mentality. When faced with adversity, I often asked, "Why is this happening to me?" I would complain, air my grievances, and continue playing the victim instead of seeing the situation as a learning opportunity.

For example, in school, both high school and college, I frequently complained about my instructors. I felt as though each one took me on a different emotional rollercoaster with peaks and valleys. I often tortured myself with negative thoughts about how hard the homework or class was. Even as I write this, those old feelings still linger. Just recently, I was supposed to attend a lecture by a well-known professor and caught myself dreading it. Instead of approaching it as a chance to walk away with a few insights, I instinctively viewed it as another obligation. This kind of thinking is deeply ingrained, years of learning to complain, rather than embracing challenges as opportunities for growth.

This habit also carried over into other parts of my life. For instance, when I encountered negative people, I didn't see it as an opportunity to learn how to manage challenging personalities. Instead, I wanted to run away. I remember someone once joked that some negative people would go to heaven and still say, "It's too bright!" That kind of constant negativity clashed with my naturally optimistic personality.

Another scenario comes to mind. Sometimes people operate under the illusion that everything they touch turns to gold, but that's rarely the case. How do you break that news to them? I worked with a colleague who constantly claimed to be the smartest person in the room, yet they frequently made critical mistakes. The demeanor suggested superiority, making it difficult to collaborate. This person hovered above correction, brushing off feedback even when it concerned significant project issues.

Every project I worked on with this person contained multiple errors, errors that went unacknowledged. Instead of confronting the situation and giving constructive feedback, I avoided working with this person as much as possible. In hindsight, I should have acknowledged the confidence while being honest about the mistakes. This approach could have improved both our working relationship and the project's outcomes. Eventually, I had to ask myself: Why is it so hard for me to work with someone like this? Maybe, just maybe, this person was placed in my life to teach me something, to help me grow in how I navigate difficult dynamics.

This realization pushed me to shift my mindset once again, from victimhood to personal growth. I started focusing on the lessons I could extract from difficult individuals and situations.

The shift in my mindset came from an unlikely source: Mariah Carey.

I was listening to an interview she did with *The Wall Street Journal*, which aired on December 11, 2020. The conversation focused on her iconic holiday hit, "All I Want for Christmas Is You," and how it evolved into the smash success we know today. When the song was first released in 1994, it received only "moderate success." But by 2020—26 twenty-six years later, it had become a defining anthem of the holiday season.

In the interview, journalist John Jurgensen called Mariah to talk about the song's transformation from modest beginnings to a cultural phenomenon. She explained that her mission was to create joyful, celebratory music for people during the holidays. While she understood the business side of music, her deeper purpose was to connect with the spirit of the season.

I was surprised to learn that Mariah wasn't initially excited about releasing a Christmas album. In the early 1990s, she was already a superstar with three hit albums and multiple chart-toppers. At the time, she thought doing a holiday album was "very premature."

Still, despite her skepticism, Mariah decided to take on the challenge. She sequestered herself in a house upstate, trying to put herself in the mood. Surrounded by lights and the usual holiday décor and "It's A Wonderful Life," the classic Jimmy Stewart Christmas movie playing in the background, she recalled, plunking out the melody on a crummy keyboard for what would become the legendary song.

As Jurgensen said, Mariah created a "timeless song" that past, present, and likely future generations will listen to, enjoy, and celebrate as part of the holiday season. Her song has been streamed over two billion times on Spotify!

By embracing her label's idea, despite her initial doubts, Mariah transformed a simple project into a cultural legacy. She is now known as the Queen of Christmas. Every year, people look forward to hearing her voice and attending her festive concerts (including me!). If she had rejected the challenge, we may never have experienced the joy and nostalgia her music brings.

Listening to that interview made me reflect on my own "Mariah Carey moments," those times when I was skeptical about a challenge, idea, or project and chose not to pursue it. How many growth opportunities have I missed simply because I didn't see them for what they were?

This realization has prompted a mindset shift that now shapes how I approach challenges and people. When I face something difficult, I ask myself three key questions:

1. Is this a window of opportunity to improve, grow, and learn?

2. What lessons can I take from this challenge that will help me succeed in the future?
3. How can I help others during their challenges so they, too, see growth opportunities in them?

This mindset has helped me transform challenges from stressors into learning experiences. It has also helped me reframe how I view professional and personal interactions that once felt draining.

About three years ago, Assistant Commissioner Lesley Hirsch interviewed me along with a panel of five people. One of her questions was whether I'd be comfortable speaking around the state and across the country. At that moment, I thought about Mariah Carey's story, how she had embraced a challenge that felt unfamiliar and, at first, unappealing. Inspired by that, I responded enthusiastically, saying I was excited for the opportunity to present and engage with different stakeholders.

Reflecting on it now, I see how that moment could have gone differently. I might have hesitated or declined. But instead, I saw it as a way to sharpen my communication skills, develop my public speaking abilities, and broaden my reach and impact.

That decision opened doors I hadn't imagined. Since then, I've been presenting at least once a week, internally, externally, across various organizations, universities, nonprofits, and businesses. It also led me to teach a course at The College of New Jersey on business statistics. I accepted the challenge not just to grow my presentation skills, but to help students see the value of statistics in everyday life.

I wanted to show them that while numbers can feel intimidating, they are also a gateway to new possibilities. Statistics help us understand everything from housing trends to personal characteristics like height and hair color. My goal was to help students see that even a tough subject can be a stepping stone to something greater.

All this happened because I took a moment to reflect, just like Mariah Carey did, and chose to lean into the challenge.

Thanks to her story, I've been able to reframe how I approach skepticism, fear, and discomfort. She was hesitant, but she pushed through. And today, she's the Queen of Christmas. Her journey reminds me that sometimes, the greatest gifts come from the opportunities we almost walked away from.

I strive to carry that same spirit into my own work and life. And I encourage you to ask yourself: How many Mariah Carey moments have you had? And how many more are waiting for you to embrace?

Sources:

Williams, Robbie. Better Man. Sing When You're Winning, Chrysalis Records, 2000. Genius, https://genius.com/Robbie-williams-better-man-lyrics.

Leimbach, Kate, and Ryan Knutson, hosts. "Happy Holidays! An Interview with the Christmas Queen." The

Journal., The Wall Street Journal, 24 Dec. 2024, https://www.wsj.com/podcasts/the-journal/happy-holidays-an-interview-with-the-christmas-queen/7919f8c8-20e5-443e-9992-6c82c88bfcfd.

All I Want for Christmas Is You by Mariah Carey." MyStreamCount, 13 Apr. 2025, https://www.mystreamcount.com/track/0bYg9bo50gSsH3LtXe2SQn. Accessed 13 Apr. 2025

LIVE IT!
Embrace the *moment*

We are all everyday changemakers – each of us contains the ability to make an impact in our own way.

What inspired Nicol to be a changemaker?

AUTHOR'S REPLY:

I believe we should all be generous in sharing our knowledge, creating an environment of collective intelligence.

NOW IT IS YOUR TURN...

What inspires you to be a changemaker?

Nicol invites you to reflect with two additional questions:

How many Mariah moments did you capitalize on?

Which Mariah moments are you still waiting to create?

Visit the "Meet the Changemakers" section at the back of the book to connect with and learn more about all of the authors featured in **LIVE IT!**

CHAPTER 15

Designed to Rise:
A Story of Resilience, Recovery & Brand
Realignment

CHANGEMAKER: DEBRA RIZZI

To my father-in-law, Staff Sergeant and Platoon Leader Joseph Rizzi, A Company, 1st Battalion, 502nd Infantry, 101st Airborne Division—whose courage in the face of paralysis and personal struggle ignited within me a deep sense of purpose and sparked the spirit of entrepreneurship that gave birth to Rizco; and to my parents, Barbara and Adrian Zapotocky, whose unwavering commitment to education and selflessness continue to inspire and guide me every day.

"We are all tested. We all come undone. But we are also all designed to rise - again and again. In that rising, we don't simply reclaim who we were; we reimagine who we're meant to become."

– DEBRA RIZZI

There are moments in life that unmake you. Moments that strip away titles, accomplishments, routines, and identities, leaving behind only the raw, trembling essence of who you are. I've unraveled more than once—but never fully broken. From standing in New York City on 9/11, becoming almost penniless during the 2008 economic crash, weathering Superstorm Sandy, and steering a company through the chaos of COVID-19, each challenge tested my capacity to lead and the strength of the brand and business I had built.

In every one of those moments, I made decisions rooted in loyalty and responsibility—often at my own expense. I prioritized the well-being of my team and the continuity of service over my own financial security. And while we're still paying for some of those sacrifices today, I wouldn't change the decisions. They shaped Rizco, my brand-led marketing agency. They shaped me.

Yet, none of those moments truly fractured my sense of self. Not until September 22, 2023. The day I was diagnosed with breast cancer.

The Unraveling

Unlike the external crises I had faced before, this was internal. Personal. Inescapable. It wasn't about saving a business or navigating a natural disaster. It was about survival—mine. It forced me to see what I had ignored for years: the toll of an overloaded schedule, too many late nights, constant client demands, emotional energy spent on relationships that didn't reciprocate, and missed moments with my own family—especially with my husband, Keith, and our three beautiful daughters, Amelia, Marley, and Monroe.

The truth is, if you don't take care of yourself, how can you truly care for others? I didn't ask, "Why me?" I knew why. The clues were there in my lifestyle, in my need to show up for everyone else while constantly pushing myself further into the background.

Cancer became the ultimate audit—the kind no brand strategist could prepare you for. It stripped everything down to the essentials: what mattered, what didn't, who showed up, and the importance of surrounding myself with the best at their craft.

Reconstructing More Than a Body

This wasn't just about a physical recovery. It was about reconstructing the leader I wanted to be. The woman. The wife. The mother. The human. I wasn't looking to bounce back—I was committed to rising differently.

Reconstruction—whether of a body, a business, or a brand—isn't a return to what was. It's a creative act of realignment. In branding, we audit. We refine. We reposition. And that's exactly what I began doing with my own life. I started evaluating every commitment, every relationship, and every energy exchange like I would a brand strategy. Is this helping us grow? Is it on message? Is this what I am supposed to be doing?

I began shifting priorities. Not just in what I said, but how I lived. More white space on the calendar. More intentional creative time. More support for my team and less pressure on myself. Less giving to people who weren't invested in my well-being. More investing in the people and causes that matter.

The Rise, Detour, and Rise Again

Recovery is rarely linear. It's a branding exercise in real-time iteration. When I first returned, I paced myself—meditating, walking, pursuing professional development, and gradually re-engaging in nonprofit leadership and volunteerism. At the six-month mark, I felt ready and was operating back at full speed.

I thought I had cleared the hardest hurdle—cancer. But healing can be deceptive when you're wired for speed. Just over a year later, chest pains, numb hands and feet, and blurred vision sent me back to the hospital. This time, the diagnosis wasn't a physical disease—it was depletion. Burnout had taken hold. Not because I was weak, but because I had defaulted to habits that no longer served me— patterns of overworking, overgiving, and undervaluing rest.

Reality Check #2

I had moved too fast. I had mistaken recovery for resolution. The lesson was clear—true healing isn't about returning to your former pace. It's about designing a sustainable rhythm that honors both your ambition and your humanity.

At that moment, I recommitted to one thing: honesty. With myself. With my family. With my team.

That honesty is fundamentally changing how we operate at Rizco. We don't just talk about work-life balance—we've built systems that respect it. We don't just suggest wellness—we're working to operationalize it. In 2024, we turned our proprietary audit process inward, surveying our own team to understand where our internal wellness stood. What we learned inspired the launch of *MOVEment*—a program focused on Mindfulness, Opportunity, Vibrancy, and Encouragement.

With the support of my incredible leadership team—Keith Rizzi, Michelle Mazur, Jill Nappi, and Alicia Shepherd—we are making real changes. We have hired additional team members to reduce overload, implemented efficiencies, and created a culture that gives explicit permission to pause—with flexible schedules, extended lunch breaks, and the space to step away when needed. We now host quarterly wellness sessions with experts who help us build a personal toolbox filled with strategies for stress management, healthy eating, and emotional resilience.

Not because it's trendy, but because it's essential. Real creativity—the kind that moves people—only flows from individuals who feel safe, seen, and whole. *MOVEment* is a living, evolving creative project—one that continues to grow alongside us.

Redefining Success

My health crisis didn't redefine my professional drive—it refined it. It stripped away the noise. Now, success is about alignment. It's about knowing the *why* behind the *what*, and being okay with walking away from opportunities that dilute your brand—or your soul.

I began asking myself bigger questions. Not just "What's next for the agency?" but "What do I want to do with my dash?"—that little line between the year you're born and the year you leave this earth, popularized by the poem *"The Dash"* by Linda Ellis. What will mine stand for?

For me, the answer is legacy. Not in the ego-driven sense, but in impact. In storytelling that matters. In continuing to mentor the next generation with a meaningful message about work-life balance. In building brands that empower— and initiatives that endure.

A Legacy of Resilience

This isn't just a personal story—it's a brand story. The brand of a woman, a leader, and a business built to bend but never break. I've walked through fire and come out not just intact, but more intentional than ever. Because every unraveling— whether personal or professional—is an invitation to rise.

We are all tested. We all come undone. But we are also all designed to rise—again and again. In that rising, we don't simply reclaim who we were; we reimagine who we're meant to become.

I don't share this story because it's unique. I share it because *transformation is universal.* Whether you're a brand, a business, or an individual—reinvention is part of the journey. And if you meet that moment with honesty, humility, and heart, the story you tell next can be your most powerful one yet.

So if you're navigating your own disruption, know this: it's not the setback that defines you. It's the identity you rebuild after. It's the brand you refine. It's the impact you choose to create.

I was designed to rise.
You are too.

LIVE IT!

Embrace the *moment*

We are all everyday changemakers – each of us contains the ability to make an impact in our own way.

What inspired Debra to be a changemaker?

AUTHOR'S REPLY:

We don't get where we are without the help of others. Just as others have done for me, it's my responsibility to continue opening doors and inspiring the next generation of leaders.

NOW IT IS YOUR TURN...

What inspires you to be a changemaker?

Debra invites you to reflect with two additional questions:

Why do I equate recovery with returning to "normal," instead of designing a rhythm that actually sustains me?

Why is it easier to sacrifice my well-being for external success than to define success on my own terms?

Visit the "Meet the Changemakers" section at the back of the book to connect with and learn more about all of the authors featured in **LIVE IT!**

CHAPTER 16

Keep
Going

_____

CHANGEMAKER: LISA CLARK

My daughters who keep me inspired when I look
at life through their eyes....

"Keep going. The next lap could
be your best one yet."

– LISA CLARK

I'm sitting alone outside at a table in Barcelona, watching the sunset and people passing by along the boardwalk as I wait for my dinner. I'm here for yet another challenging and highly competitive race this weekend. Although they say age is just a number, the sport takes its toll mentally and physically.

This fast track I am on is motorsport racing—high-powered and fast cars, racing all over the planet with people sharing this crazy, high-risk passion. Steve McQueen once said, "Racing is life. Anything that happens before or after is just waiting." That phrase has resonated with me since the beginning of finding this passion.

I've been told that I am the oldest female race car driver in the sport. It's a thought I really embrace. Even being a female in a male-dominated sport doesn't dominate my thoughts. I just did it. It was—and still is—a self-fulfilling challenge to myself. I guess after doing it, I realized it was drawing attention from others.

This was my journey. I didn't want to have to focus on having to show up for anyone else. But when you are out there and people start to tell you that you're inspiring others, it becomes a responsibility to give back. It was then that I realized I am now making a difference, not just for myself but for others. That gives this life a whole new meaning.

This passion carried from this journey I've been on gives me an inner purpose and feeds my soul. It takes no prisoners and can drain you to the core. It takes away all your self-esteem and then blesses you with the moment of self-fulfilled glory and addiction that seems to check all the boxes.

Having memories of being raised by a single dad in a blue-collar lifestyle, there were lots of struggles along the way. But it never occurred to me to quit at anything I pursued. I was raised to believe you work hard, no matter what the cost and sacrifice, as the only way to build yourself.

So here I am, years later, having made many sacrifices along the way to be here in this moment. There are painful moments when you don't think there is a way to come back into the light again. But you keep going, allowing yourself to take another step, trying to find a mental place within yourself and focus on the rebuilding of what took you down. Keep going.

Being committed to a marriage, raising a family, and building a business were a big part of my life for thirty years. The plan was to enjoy the fruits of the labor with my partner. But life seems to change things in an instant, and the floor dropping out from under you is a hard one to recover from. Another emotional trauma that you don't see happening—but you recover and try to find that safe place inside yourself. A place that allows you to heal and then take that step outside of yourself and find a path. Keep going again. Keep the keep going.

This sport gave me a purpose to better myself and challenge myself. I wasn't doing it for anybody else but myself, and that alone strengthened my focus to keep going.

I've been in a race car now for over ten years. So many ups and downs, with many tears involved. But the satisfaction overwhelms pretty much everything else that life has to offer at this point. The exploration of life never ends. I keep going. Something inside me tells me that there is more purpose to be found.

There is a flame inside that I felt was ignited as a young girl when I felt I had no one to make me okay but myself. Finding something to strive for gives you inner confidence that you will be okay. The feeling of working hard at something makes the sacrifice seem all worth it. Such a strong force pushes aside the fear of failing.

So much more, when you have built this inner strength, you're less concerned about what others think about you. You start to realize their judgments really seem to carry less impact. Finding that zone for yourself is an energizing feeling. It's where you grow and feel much satisfaction with the path that you're on. That pushes you to keep going.

We all have our childhood traumas and memories that we carry within ourselves. They always say you need to work through them to heal from your own. Finding something that gives me a focal point and immersing myself in racing does that for me. It puts me in a place that allows me to put those memories in a box and be thankful for being able to move forward. That's what makes us who we are.

The battle scars and wounds give us the strength to believe in ourselves and know that we will be okay. Closing the door on those painful memories and allowing ourselves to know that life doesn't end with them—it keeps going. I keep going.

I feel this path I've been on is winding down. I feel some resistance to pushing the limit. I don't want to fight this feeling, but at the same time, maybe it's giving me a new challenge. I keep listening to that voice inside and learn how to get along with it. The complexity of the soul—and what drives us and holds us back to protect us—is sometimes hard to listen to.

I always want to be better, do better, and keep moving into becoming more of what I think I am capable of. Otherwise, what's the point of going through life just to reach a finish line without trophies for yourself? I don't think we were put here to go through the motions, but rather to feel pain, joy, sacrifice, and love. Racing has given me all those experiences.

You carry a mutual understanding of this with people involved in the sport. Having that camaraderie has helped me get to where I am. They have shared the same intensity of knowing the obstacles and challenges, and having shared in the accolades of success. It's again the fire inside of me that keeps burning, keeps us going.

Choosing this path for myself has changed the dynamics of some friendships. It becomes a hard transition after being on the road racing and then coming back into what people call a normal life. It can become a bit lonesome, as you are now with friends who have been moving forward in their daily lives, but the commonality is different. They want to hear your stories about how the race went. They try to understand the experience, but I can tell by the look in their eyes that it's a distant interest. Sometimes the feeling is mutual. Sometimes it just feels good to come back home and hibernate, get the tasks and errands caught up, and then get back out on the road again as soon as I can. That is my true comfort zone.

It's hard to imagine a future without being in a race car. The preparation, anticipation, and process of getting prepared with a full calendar for ten months each year of racing will be a hard drug to quit. Each competitor wants to be better, do better each race week. The support from the team we race with and my coach means a lot. The relationship with the crew is vital.

I recently had brake failure. You're going at about 160 miles per hour into a brake zone. When that happens, you definitely see life flash before your eyes. I fixate on those moments sometimes. But I keep going.

Opening season of 2021, first test of the year—I had a bad crash in Daytona and ended up in the hospital for ten days. A painful and gut-wrenching time, as I had just gone through a divorce and was just back on my feet, bringing it to a new chapter of myself. It was a setback in my confidence and understanding of "why me?"

I remember when the call was made to my daughters that I had been in a crash. I was okay, but in the hospital. One flew over right away, and when she came and saw me there, she said, "Mom, you are done. No more racing." And she started to cry.

I had no idea it was impacting her the way it was. But it wasn't an option for me to quit racing at that point. All I could think about was how fast I would heal so I could get back into that race car. I tried to explain to her that racing wasn't finished with me yet. I had to be the one to decide when I would stop racing. This had to be my decision and on my terms. I had come too far, worked too hard, sacrificed too much to call it quits just yet. And so the healing began, and within six months, I was back in a race car.

There's an endless strength we all carry within ourselves, but there are scars that will remain. When you're in a race car, focus is intense. Being challenged by many factors, learning how to manage the chaos of thoughts—those scars can come into play. For me, I have a memory of the pain in the moments before the crash. Fear becomes a factor, and learning how to manage that fear and channel it into a driving force in a race car can be a great tool. It can also be a hindrance if not handled properly.

Motorsport isn't just something I do. It's part of who I am.

As a female driver, I know I carry more than just my own ambitions onto the track. I carry the hopes of every woman who's ever been told she's too old, too fragile, or that her time has passed.

But the truth is, I'm not finished. I still have more to give, more to learn, and more to chase. The theme that drives me on and off the track is simple: keep going.

No matter the season of life, no matter the noise around you, you keep going. My reflexes may have matured, my mindset may have deepened, but my competitive spirit is sharper than ever.

I show up because I can, because I want to, and because I still believe in the power of forward motion.

I'm not ready to stop—not when I know there are people who believe in me, people who are inspired by my persistence, and even those who rely on my presence in the paddock. Whether it's the younger drivers I mentor, the teams who've grown with me, or the fans who've followed my journey, I feel a responsibility to stay in it.

I want to be a living reminder that passion doesn't retire, and grit doesn't age. I race to prove that just because something gets harder doesn't mean it's time to quit.

The story isn't over just because the road gets rougher. If anything, it's the bumps that make the journey worth telling.

So, I keep driving.
I keep pushing.
And I keep showing myself what's possible.

LIVE IT!
Embrace the *moment*

We are all everyday changemakers – each of us contains the ability to make an impact in our own way.

What inspired Lisa to be a changemaker?

AUTHOR'S REPLY:
What inspires me to be a changemaker is watching those who have taken the leap to step outside their comfort zones. This has helped me gain the confidence of knowing failure is part of the process. Now, I find it easier for me to get back up and try again with less fear.

NOW IT IS YOUR TURN...

What inspires you to be a changemaker?

Lisa invites you to reflect with two additional questions:

What is it that sparks hope in you for the journey ahead?

How can you be more open to look for those moments to step outside of your comfort zone?

Visit the "Meet the Changemakers" section at the back of the book to connect with and learn more about all of the authors featured in **LIVE IT!**

CHAPTER 17

Flip
the Script

CHANGEMAKER: CATHERINE CURRY-WILLIAMS

Dedicated to my daughter, Grace, and every young
woman who deserves a world where flipping the
script isn't radical—it's routine.

"When I was young, I heard the saying, 'If not me, who? If not now, when?' It hit me like a lightning bolt. It taught me that waiting for permission or perfect timing is a losing game. That quote has fueled everything I've done, from building playgrounds where every kid belongs to flipping the script on how we fund women's dreams."

– CATHERINE CURRY-WILLIAMS

*I*f you know me, you know I'm the kind of person who sees a problem and says, "Hold my coffee, I've got this." I never set out to be an authority on feminism or philanthropy— I just saw gaps and got pissed off enough to do something about them. After almost three decades, I've had more "aha" moments than I can count, each one teaching me that real change happens when we refuse to play by old rules.

Building sensory-rich, literacy-friendly playgrounds around the world taught me that inclusion isn't a bonus; it's the whole point. In 1997, I founded Shane's Inspiration to break down the barriers that keep children with disabilities apart from typically abled kids. Yet, as I watched women-led groups, after-school STEM clubs, and girls' mentorship programs stumble over the funding hurdles, I knew I had to flip another script. So in 2020, I co-founded She Angels Foundation to channel collective giving into grassroots, female-founded nonprofits. Along the way, as an activist, mother, sister, aunt, wife, and friend, I earned what I like to call a PhD in life: one paid for in scraped knees, late-night board meetings, and countless "aha" moments.

I wasn't born knowing what it meant to be a woman or an activist; I became both by facing down obstacles, rewriting the rules I'd inherited, and claiming my own story.

Flipping the script isn't a women-only play; it's every daughter, son, sister, and brother showing up for the mothers and friends they love. Feminism is about learning from the past and making things better by listening to those who came before us, learning from missteps, and speaking up when silence no longer serves. So here's your call to action: what's the piece of wisdom you carry, and how will you bring it to life for yourself and for the people who matter most? Because real change happens the second we turn insight into impact.

"Someday Is Now" The Reality of Charitable Giving in the US

You know how we all say, "Someday, when I have more time...Someday, when I have more money...Someday...?" Well, newsflash: **Someday is now.** Especially when it comes to how we give. Because right now, in the richest country on Earth, our charitable dollars are doing some really weird things.

These numbers are from the Lilly Family School of Philanthropy at Indiana University, the organization that first exposed the disparity in how little women and girls actually receive. Here's the rough breakdown of **every dollar** Americans give to charity:

- **29%** to religious organizations
- **12%** to education (hello, college endowments!)
- **14%** to human services (food banks, domestic violence shelters)
- **9%** to health
- **7%** to international causes
- **5%** to arts & culture
- **3–4%** to the environment & animals
- **1.8%** to women & girls

Pause. Let that sink in.

- **Animals** get more than women and girls.
- **Women and girls**, who make up **over half** the population, get **less than two cents** of every charitable dollar.

That's not just a "huh", it's a **kick-in-the-gut moment**. Here's the real talk,no lectures, just straight-up truth.

1. **Old Boys' Club Vibe**
   - Big donors and foundation boards have historically been **mostly men**, funding causes they know, think church building, college endowments, sports stadiums. Women's issues are often invisible.
2. Invisible Work Gets Invisible Money
   - Women-led groups fix problems you don't hear about on the news, like teaching financial literacy to single moms or running after-school STEM clubs for girls. Because nobody's shouting about it, it doesn't make those sexy stats that funders love.
3. Unconscious Bias
   - Even the nicest people carry "invisible filters." They might think, *"Oh, food banks are important, but that women's mentorship program is kind of niche."* That bias stacks up.
4. Size and Speed
   - Grassroots groups often run on a shoestring, no six-figure salaries or fancy marketing. Big

foundations say, *"We need audited financials and five-year plans."* Small outfits can't keep up with the paperwork, so they miss out.

What's wrong with all this?

- **It's Unfair.** Over half the world's brainpower, creativity, and sweat go underfunded.
- **It's Stupid.** When women thrive, **communities thrive**, kids do better in school, local economies hum, and neighborhoods get safer. Shorting women is like chopping off a whole arm of society.
- **It Holds Us Back.** If we ignore half the population, we're slamming the brakes on progress, on health, education, the environment, everything that makes life better for everyone.

Facts on women-led businesses

Studies show that women-led businesses often inspire more loyalty and trust. For example, companies with women in executive roles see 10% higher returns on equity, according to MSCI World Research. Edelman's Trust Barometer found that businesses with more gender-diverse leadership enjoy increased trust. Research from the *Harvard Business Review* also highlights consumer preferences for brands that support diversity. Additionally, Great Place to Work, the global authority on workplace culture, found that gender-diverse companies have 5-10% higher employee retention rates. These are great facts to reference!

Research supports that women-led companies tend to be more profitable. For example, McKinsey & Company's "Diversity Matters" report (2015) found that companies with a gender-diverse workforce were 15% more likely to outperform financially. Other data shows companies with 30% female executives seeing a 6% higher net profit margin, while those with women CFOs generate 76% higher returns. Studies also show that women-owned businesses often secure more funding and demonstrate better ROI and longevity. Trust in businesses increases when leadership includes women, according to the Edelman Trust Barometer, a global communication resource many have turned to for twenty-five years.

Data shows companies with **more women in leadership** have up to a **30% lower turnover** and report **higher employee satisfaction**.

- **Catalyst (2019)** found that having women in senior roles boosts team innovation by **20–30%**.

In plain English: **we're wasting talent and stopping good things from happening.**

"Why fund women?" **It's plain to see:** When women lead, the company makes more money.

People stick with and spend more on brands they trust to treat women fairly. When women lead, employees feel more connected and tend to stay longer. And that's why **Someday Is Now**, let's flip the script, fund women and girls, and watch the magic unfold.

Here's how we "flip the switch" and make real change happen: Grantmakers need to add to their playbook

1. **Rolling Deadlines**
   Why: Emergencies don't wait for grant season.
   How: Accept applications all year long, so grassroots groups can apply the minute they need money.

2. **Micro-Grants ($1K–$10K)**
   Why: Spark new ideas and cover urgent costs without drowning small groups in paperwork.
   How: Offer a "quick cash" lane specifically for women-led initiatives, no PhD in grant writing required.

3. **Fast Decisions (30 days)**
   Why: When a shelter's roof leaks or a tutoring center needs winter coats, time is everything.
   How: Commit to a yes/no in four weeks.

4. **Unrestricted Funding**
   Why: Nonprofits sometimes need rent, utilities, or a new laptop more than a shiny program budget line.
   How: Let grantees decide their biggest needs. Trust them to be the experts in their own communities.

5. **Simplified Applications**
   Why: The biggest barrier to funding is often the application itself.
   How: Swap endless forms for a two-page online form.

What Individual Donors Can Do Today

1. **Give $1.40 a Day**
   Why: It's less than your streaming bill, yet pooled with ten others in one year, it becomes enough to give a **$5K grant** to a community organization.
   How: Start a giving circle with your friend group. Ten friends pool their donations of $1.40 a day, equaling $5K a year.

2. **Amplify Women's Voices**
   Why: Awareness leads to action (and more donors!).
   How: Share a woman's leadership story and its effects on social media; then tag friends.

3. **Volunteer Smart**
   Why: Time is just as precious as money.
   How: Offer your skills, marketing, bookkeeping, whatever, to a local women's group for a few hours each month.

4. **Champion at Work**
   Why: Workplace matches and corporate grants can double your impact.
   How: Ask HR if your gift can be matched. Suggest a "Women's Impact Fund" for colleagues to join.

There you have it. Flip the script by doing something today, whatever you have time, skills, or a couple of bucks. Because **someday** is now, and the story we write next is up to us.

LIVE IT!

Embrace the *moment*

We are all everyday changemakers – each of us contains the ability to make an impact in our own way.

What inspired Catherine to be a changemaker?

AUTHOR'S REPLY:

I've seen too many gaps and too many "somedays." I believe even small acts can spark big change. I'm driven by passion, grit, hope, and the belief that collective voices, and actions, can rewrite the rules.

NOW IT IS YOUR TURN...

What inspires you to be a changemaker?

Catherine invites you to reflect with two additional questions:

What's one small action you'll take this week to push your "someday" into now?

Where in your life do you see a gap that needs your voice, and what's stopping you from speaking up?

Visit the "Meet the Changemakers" section at the back of the book to connect with and learn more about all of the authors featured in **LIVE IT!**

LIVE IT! *reflection*

Passion Meets Purpose

---

*"Your best life begins when what you
love becomes what you give."*

– ANN MARIE BAKER

When I was ten years old, I would lose myself for hours with a
paintbrush in my hand. Art was my escape, my joy, and my voice. That
love carried me through high school, college, and into a forty-year
career at an award-winning advertising agency. I never imagined that
my childhood passion would one day become a way to serve others in
the most meaningful way.

Years ago, a friend asked if I would join a marketing committee for a
nonprofit. I said yes without hesitation, not realizing how deeply that
"yes" would shape my life. One committee led to another, and soon I was
serving on multiple nonprofit boards and advisory committees.

I discovered something profound—my skills, my creativity, and my
business experience could be a lifeline for organizations doing incredible
work with little to no resources. Through my role at Design 446, I could

tell their stories, promote their missions, and give them tools they never had access to. Today, we serve over thirty for-impact organizations.

The greatest reward for me comes when I receive an email that says, "Thank you for all the wonderful ways you have elevated our presence, and the difference you created in changing our perception, your insight and wisdom has been nothing short of miraculous!" In those moments, I know I've found the purpose behind my passion.

Art gave me a career. Service gave me meaning. Today, I am deeply grateful that the gift I found as a little girl can now be given back to help and to inspire those who need it most. When passion meets purpose, the real impact happens!

Ann Marie invites you to reflect on these two questions:

What is your passion?

How can you share your passion to benefit someone else?

CHAPTER 18

Finding Meaning in

Grief

CHANGEMAKER: JENNIFER DEVI CHAUHAN

My chapter is dedicated to
Judith & Patrick Chauhan

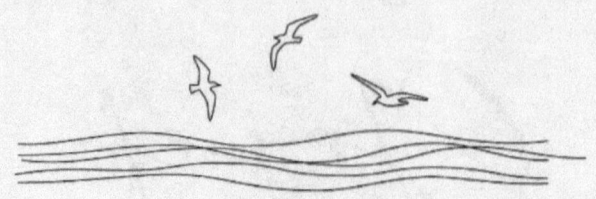

"Your story matters, and you are the only
one who can tell it."

– JENNIFER DEVI CHAUHAN

I headed up the staircase and down the hall—taking note of the steel steps, the white brick walls, the vaulted ceilings—until we came to the room I had rented in an industrial-style building in Red Bank, New Jersey. It was even better than the photo my friend, who worked for the landlord, had shown me on her phone.

A single room, it had tall windows, brick walls, wide-plank wooden floors, and a metal ladder leading up to a tiny loft. It was the perfect spot to launch the nonprofit I had been slowly building. I could already see it—different groups of people, all ages, sitting around a large table, pens in hand, writing stories and poems in their notebooks. I wanted to create a space where people could come together and be celebrated for who they are—for their experiences, thoughts, and dreams.

But even more, I wanted to do something to honor the memory of my mother, who passed away seven years earlier. Who told me at a young age that I could do anything if I believed in myself. Who told me when I was an adolescent struggling with anxiety: "Go write." I became a writer because of her, and I wanted to give that opportunity to as many people as possible.

My mother's death had devastated me.

In March 2007, she called as I was hustling my three children—ages six, four, and two—into our house after picking my oldest up from dance class.

"Jen, they found a mass," she said.

I shifted the phone to my other ear and scooted my children into the den.

"A what?"

"An ill-defined mass in my lungs."

I immediately went into problem-solving mode, not allowing any emotion to penetrate. I made doctor's appointments at Sloan Kettering. I found an apartment in a nearby town to move my mother (and my father, who was twenty years her senior and already battling a terminal illness) from Maryland closer so I could become her primary caregiver. I found a babysitter on Craigslist to help take care of my children.

Saving her became my sole focus. Even when the chemo treatments weren't working, even when her lungs filled with fluid and we were in and out of the hospital multiple times a week to drain them, even when six months later I had to sign her into hospice after an emergency procedure failed.

She was too young, age sixty-four, when she passed away days later as I held her hand, at the height of her career as a director of HR for a government nonprofit. She was Grammy, a woman who loved my children as much as I did. She was my best friend, the person I called every day at 5:30 p.m. as I was making dinner and she was cleaning up her desk.

How was I going to survive without her?

Her death became the unraveling of my life as I knew it. Overwhelmed with grief, I muddled through my days doing the best I could to pack lunches, shuttle the kids to their activities, and sit through dinners with friends. I found my tolerance for small talk dwindling. How could everyone keep moving about their lives as if nothing had happened?

I also became the primary caregiver for my father, who passed away a year and a half later in April 2008 from pulmonary fibrosis. After his death, the fog descended even more. I couldn't hold onto thoughts, words jumbling in and out of comprehension. I became fatigued, and my joints started aching. Was I depressed?

At my annual physical in August, while filling out paperwork, my breathing suddenly became shallow, and my heart began racing as I marked my parents deceased in the family history section. My doctor informed me I'd had a panic attack and handed me a card for a therapist specializing in bereavement. I called to make an appointment as soon as I got in my car.

In the weeks that followed, the fatigue and joint pain became so debilitating that I could barely get out of bed. I feared I had some type of cancer or other terminal illness. My doctor ran tests, and the bloodwork came back off the charts for Celiac Disease. They scheduled an emergency endoscopy, which confirmed I did have the autoimmune disorder in which eating gluten triggers the immune system to damage the small intestine. All the villi had flattened, and I was not absorbing any nutrients.

During this time, I could feel other parts of my life falling apart, too. My husband was growing more distant, spending more time at work and away from home. About six months later, he moved out to New York City, and we decided to divorce.

I had no idea what I was going to do. I was alone with three small children—now nine, seven, and five. With my parents gone and my brothers living across the country, I had no family nearby to help. I had no job to rely on, having left my teaching position when I was pregnant with my third child and giving up my tenured spot when my mom was first diagnosed.

I wanted to run away and even entertained the thought of moving to California to be closer to my younger brother, but my divorce agreement wouldn't permit leaving the state without my ex's permission.

At one of my weekly therapy sessions, my therapist told me, "Create the life you want right here."

But what did I want?

When you are stripped of the only life you've known, the future you had imagined, you have no choice but to go inward. To get comfortable with being exactly where you are, no matter how painful and alone you may feel.

During one of the early days of hospice, I had climbed into my mother's hospital bed and asked her, "How will I do this without you?"

"My death will make you a better writer," she had said.

I opened a journal and started pouring all my feelings—my anger, my frustration, my sadness, my grief—into the pages. I wrote while sitting in my car—waiting to pick a child up from school, from an activity, from a playdate. I wrote late at night, after the kids were tucked in bed, our tiny rental house hushed in darkness. The only hour I had all to myself.

I knew I needed to heal myself, to figure out who I was and what I really wanted out of my life. I also knew I wanted flexibility, so I could be available for my young children. As much as I couldn't afford not to get a full-time job, I also couldn't afford to be in a job that could be physically taxing and emotionally toxic. I was fortunate that I was getting alimony (although it was nowhere near enough to support a family of four).

I thought about what I loved to do most: write and teach writing. My career began as an education journalist, which inspired me to go to grad school to become a teacher. After graduation, I worked for a nonprofit teaching writing to teens in the foster care system of New York City. When I got married and moved to the Jersey Shore, I took a job as a high school English and Creative Writing teacher.

As a classroom teacher, something unexpected had happened. I didn't realize it at the time, but I was conducting an unofficial experiment. Even though I was teaching writing in all my classes, the creative writing students were responding differently. They were walking into class excited to put pen to paper. They were writing authentically, exploring their voices, and taking risks. I also noticed how close they had become through sharing their writing, building a trusting community. They knew personal things about each other, and it made them more compassionate and kinder to one another. I realized this is how all children should experience writing, not just kids in my elective.

I thought about my mom and her mantra: "If you're on this planet, make a difference."

One day, the idea for a nonprofit, "Project Write Now," popped into my head. I imagined a studio space where people of all ages, but especially youth, could come to write. I kept hearing a voice, a whispering, telling me to give back. I remembered how healing writing and sharing their stories had been for the teens in foster care. I knew I wanted to partner with schools and mission-driven nonprofits to bring expressive writing programs to as many people as possible. I wanted to build a community around the healing and connective power of storytelling.

Fortunately, I met two other people with similar passions and interests who joined me in creating the organization. We came up with a model that would have a fee-based revenue stream through paid classes. Then we'd have outreach programs that would offer creative and expressive writing experiences for free for underserved communities.

When we opened the doors to that cool little space in the industrial building in Red Bank in September 2014, we had only one class with three adults and no community outreach partners. But I wasn't discouraged. I knew we had to start somewhere. I began building relationships with school administrators and directors of other nonprofits, offering our programs.

At the time, friends and family, meaning well, would ask me: "What do you know about running a nonprofit?" My answer: "Nothing." The only business classes I'd taken were two economics courses while an undergrad.

But this felt like a calling. Like I couldn't stop even if I wanted to.

Little by little, our classes began growing, and we connected with the local middle school, creating a yearlong weekly expressive writing program for seventh and eighth graders in the AVID (Advancement Via Individual Determination) program that is still going strong.

Today, we have a team of four full-time employees and dozens of instructors. We run more than forty six-week classes a year for hundreds of adults, along with one-day workshops and community storytelling events. When the pandemic forced us to give up our space, we moved most programs online, which allowed us to welcome participants from across the country and beyond. Five years ago, we launched a book-writing program for novelists and memoirists, and several of our writers will see their books published next year.

Our community outreach programs have flourished as more people discover the transformative benefits of expressive writing. We now partner with thirty-five to forty schools and mission-driven organizations annually, and we've impacted more than 12,000 youth and adults to date.

One of the programs closest to my heart began in 2021 in India, my father's home country. A teen from India who found us on Instagram began interning with us and was Zooming into a program we were running for middle school students at the Asbury Park unit of the Boys & Girls Clubs of Monmouth County. She loved it so much that she asked if we could create something similar in her country. With her support, we've launched six-week programs for children, teens, adults, and teachers in India. I lead the adult journaling program and spend Friday mornings with a group of women in India, which has brought me so much joy. It has reconnected me to my heritage in a way I thought I had lost when my father passed.

Over the years, my belief in the power of expressive writing has only strengthened. It gives us a meaningful way to process emotions, clarify our thoughts, and, most importantly, uncover our authentic selves. Studies prove expressive writing reduces stress and improves mood, but I've also seen how it helps people quiet the noise of the world around them so they can discover their voices and connect to what matters most to them.

Always a student and wanting to deepen my inner work, in 2023, I earned a 200-hour inclusive, trauma-informed mindfulness, social-emotional learning, and yoga certification. I've seen so much synergy between expressive writing and yoga, and I hope to develop more programs that combine these practices.

I know it sounds dramatic, but creating Project Write Now saved me by helping me find meaning in my grief. It gave me a space to rediscover who I am and to heal from tremendous loss. It has also helped me create and deepen relationships with so many people. My team, yes, but also all the community partners, their students/clients, and others who take classes or attend our events. People of all ages, backgrounds, and experiences, I would have never met had I not gone on this journey.

A journey in which I get to honor my mother's memory every day by giving others what she gave me—a supportive space to be valued for who you are and for your story.

LIVE IT!
Embrace the *moment*

We are all everyday changemakers – each of us contains the ability to make an impact in our own way.

What inspired Jennifer to be a changemaker?

AUTHOR'S REPLY:
The people I connect with every day inspire me. I've been so fortunate to meet so many incredible people whose stories have touched my heart. I believe that everyone is a writer because everyone has a story to tell. I want to give people opportunities to share their stories so they can experience the healing power of writing.

NOW IT IS YOUR TURN...

What inspires you to be a changemaker?

Jennifer invites you to reflect with two additional questions:

When was the last time you opened up a journal or a blank document on your computer and just wrote? Not for anyone but yourself?

What is the story only you can tell?

Visit the "Meet the Changemakers" section at the back of the book to connect with and learn more about all of the authors featured in **LIVE IT!**

CHAPTER 19

Recognizing
the Changemaker in Me

CHANGEMAKER: TARA COFFMAN

To my daughter, Abigail, who inspires me to
be better every single day.

"It's never too late to make a change, to start over, to reinvent yourself, to do the right thing."

– TARA COFFMAN

As humans, changemaking is in our DNA. Throughout time, as we have evolved, we have transformed our surroundings, ourselves, those around us, and our environment. Our very humanity gives us the will and ability to *make change*. And even so, our ability to change isn't something most of us think about as a power we possess. In fact, in my experience, most of us lament how hard change is, or how little impact the changes we make have on a grander scale. In thinking about the concept of change and changemaking during the process of writing this chapter, my own ideas about change have evolved, and I've come to think about it in a new light. I've come to see myself as a changemaker where I didn't before.

Big "C", Little "c" Changemakers

When I thought about what it means to be a Changemaker, I thought about people like Martin Luther King Jr., Ruth Bader Ginsburg, or Oprah Winfrey. People who made an impact on a grand scale, reaching millions of people and transforming the world. I would argue, however, that underneath monumental Changemaking is an undercurrent of changemaking which, like a ripple in the ocean, builds and grows into something much greater and more impactful. That, in fact, we can all be changemakers on the most granular level, within ourselves, our families, and our communities.

The more I thought about it, the more I realized that I am a little "c" changemaker—and that can be just as important as being a big "C" Changemaker. I haven't necessarily done anything monumental to transform the world at large, but I have worked to embrace change in my own life in little ways that will hopefully create small ripples of change through those I touch and have an impact on. In the ways I've navigated transformation in my identity, career, and family, I have come to see myself as a changemaker. Whether it's working on my mental health with therapy, encouraging my kids to live authentically and with purpose, or building a career from scratch in my fifties, I have made changes in myself, and hopefully in my family and community, that will carry on with future generations and become part of greater change in the world.

In writing this chapter, I hope that you are inspired to recognize and embrace the changemaker in yourself. I want you to realize the impact that little changes can have on yourself, your family, and your community. I want you to recognize that making a pivot, adapting to one's environment, creating something new, or improving what is, are all important ways of being a changemaker in your own life and the lives of those you touch. In my own life, I have worked to make changes in myself—in the way I see myself, the way I value myself, and in how I show up both in the world and for my family. I've learned to embrace change, or at least not to resist it, and to understand that in a way, the only certain thing in life is that things will change—both in ways we control and in ways we don't. I have worked to transform myself into someone who values and embraces change both in myself and others.

Young Changemakers

I remember distinctly as a girl, having conversations with my best friend, Lisa, about what we would be when we grew up. As young teenagers, we talked of being career women—veterinarians, lawyers, even president, but we always came back to the question of what would happen to our careers when we were ready to start a family. Even at that young age, we sensed the difficulty of balancing career and family. How would we navigate building successful careers with the desire to stay home and raise our future children? How would we take five years or more out of our careers and still be "successful" professionals? We realized then that something would have to change—*we* would have to change. In imagining our future, we knew we would have to adapt—from career women to homemakers and then back again to career women, transforming and remaking ourselves along the way.

One of the greatest motivators for change in my younger years was my relationship with my mother. As far back as I can remember, we had a difficult relationship. Looking back, I'm certain she struggled with depression and anxiety, and she was certainly terrified of change. I felt responsible for her mood swings and her unhappiness, and no matter what I did, I couldn't change our relationship. We had different personality types, and I didn't understand at the time why she seemed unhappy with me most of the time. We fought often, and I felt I could never please her, that I was invisible and unimportant. I often struggled with depression myself, and I felt that things would never change, never get better, until I could get out on my own. In this phase, I learned about the power of change, how change could bring freedom and relief. I came to realize that you can never change another person—only how you react to them. This was the change I sought after high school and through college. It was a period when I worked to change my situation, but it would be quite a few years before I started the larger task of changing myself.

Once I started college and then began working full-time, I didn't think much about becoming a Changemaker. I was focused much more on the short term and not the big picture. Working, studying, and gaining independence from my parents all took precedence and made my focus much smaller. The transformation I was focused on during this time was in my own life. My actions were much more granular; my focus was only on the next thing. I knew, however, that I would create change for myself by going out on my own and living my life on my terms—that this was the path that would allow me to eventually create the changes I wanted within myself. I knew that once I started my own family, I would somehow not do the things my parents did; that I couldn't alter the past, but through my future actions, I could transform my life going forward. I graduated from college, started a career, and got married before change came and punched me in the gut.

Growing into Change

My first real experience with changemaking came with my first marriage and divorce. I didn't realize it at the time, but

I was suddenly forced to change. Although I resisted it with my entire being, I did change. As human beings, we're wired to adapt both through adversity and success. I did something I felt at the time would be impossible—I started over in my thirties. I took so many things that I hadn't wanted—feeling like a failure, starting over, being alone, being divorced—and transformed them into something new. I changed my life into something I *did* want—a new job, a family, a new marriage, a new home. It was then that I realized I could pivot. I could overcome the worst thing I could imagine and create a life and a family I had only dreamed of. The lesson I learned through this time was that change was inevitable and not always in my control, but that I could survive it. I learned that I could even harness change and make it work to my advantage. I discovered that my power was not in resisting change, but in accepting and even embracing change and using it to grow and evolve.

I see this era of my life as changemaking through pivoting— adapting and changing to whatever was best for my family, my kids, my marriage. I pivoted from stay-at-home mom to working mom and continued to morph as my family's needs changed. Whether it was working the midnight shift to maximize income and be there for the kids or taking small promotions to increase my income without sacrificing family time, these years were a constant balancing act to hold it all together. This era of changemaking was also focused on making changes in how I related to my kids in relation to how I was raised. This was perhaps my most important change to date. I worked to show my kids unconditional love and acceptance. I worked to treat them with equality and fairness, and to be present and joyful with them as they grew and learned. I worked to be the parent for my kids that I had needed as a child. It remains to be seen whether I've succeeded, but I am confident that I did my very best for them and hope to have made a change for future generations.

It was in these years of raising my kids that I worked to be a changemaker by working on my mental health - managing my anxiety and staying present with my family to create the loving environment that I missed growing up. I worked hard during these years to be a stable, loving, safe place for my family. I am a changemaker in my family, working to break the stigma of mental illness and building skills to pass on to my kids around mental health, communication skills, and what it means to love someone. I've worked hard to maintain open, honest communication with my kids and to encourage them to trust in themselves and be true to themselves. I'm far from perfect, but I'm showing my kids that the most important thing is to try—to try to work on myself, to do the best I can for my family, to always try to be better each and every day.

Changemaking as Reinvention

Now that my kids are almost grown, I'm embracing changemaking as reinvention once again, but this time on my terms. Still prioritizing family, but working on a career for the first time and building something for myself and my future. I'm working on becoming more of a Changemaker through my work as a financial professional and leaning into the power of helping others and making positive changes for other families. I'm looking at changemaking with a broader point of view—working to make a bigger impact and realizing that it's never too late to embrace change on a larger scale. I'm learning to be a Changemaker by giving up control and taking chances, by trusting myself and my abilities and instincts.

As I embark on this latest chapter in my journey, I'm more mindful of making and embracing change and encouraging change in those around me. Starting a new career in my fifties, encouraging my husband on his journey into retirement, guiding my kids into the world, and starting their own journey toward independence. I'm realizing that our lives are changing all the time and that change is the beauty of life. The truth is that we are all changing all the time— some of it purposefully and with intention, and some of it random and unnoticed. As I'm aging, I find comfort in the fact that change is the only real constant. Everything will ultimately change, and we are at times changemakers and Changemakers to varying degrees. Anyone can be a changemaker, putting positivity into the world in as many ways as possible. True changemaking is breaking patterns of dysfunction that have been handed down through families—to create a space for positivity and love to flourish on any scale.

LIVE IT!

Embrace the *moment*

We are all everyday changemakers – each of us contains the ability to make an impact in our own way.

What inspired Tara to be a changemaker?

AUTHOR'S REPLY:
I used to think being a changemaker meant doing big, world-changing things. But over time, I've realized that being a changemaker can also mean making small, everyday choices that make a difference. I've seen how even little actions can create ripples of change, and that inspires me to keep growing, learning, and doing my part to make the world around me a little better each day.

NOW IT IS YOUR TURN...

What inspires you to be a changemaker?

Tara invites you to reflect with two additional questions:

Do you see yourself as a changemaker? In what way(s)?

What inspires you to make changes in your life, family, and community?

Visit the "Meet the Changemakers" section at the back of the book to connect with and learn more about all of the authors featured in **LIVE IT!**

CHAPTER 20

Using Your Own Crayon to Draw Out Your Journey

CHANGEMAKER: HELEN ARCHONTOU, MSW, LSW

To the next generation of leaders—especially my
children, Julia and Steven—with the hope that they
practice healthy boundaries and behaviors
for themselves while they work to build a more just
and compassionate world for all.

"Bravery is showing up with some fear
and some faith."

– HELEN ARCHONTOU, MSW, LSW

*L*eadership, particularly in the nonprofit and social justice space, is not for the faint-hearted. It's filled with setbacks, doubts, and moments where the odds seem insurmountable. Over the years, as the CEO of YWCA Northern New Jersey and a passionate advocate for equity, I've faced my share of challenges—from managing crises and funding gaps to advocating for policy changes and representing marginalized voices. What has helped me not just endure, but lead with clarity and resilience, are two simple, yet profoundly transformative practices: **positive self-talk** and **visualization**.

They've helped me lead with confidence, resilience, and clarity—even when the path ahead felt uncertain. These aren't practices just for CEOs, though; they are for *anyone* who wants to live a more grounded, impactful, and intentional life.

Before "growth mindset" became a buzzword and long before self-help books filled the shelves, *The Little Engine That Could* quietly delivered one of the most important life lessons we can learn: the power of what we say to ourselves has everything to do with outcomes.

At its core, *The Little Engine That Could* is a manual for positive self-talk dressed up as a children's book. When the little blue engine faces a seemingly impossible challenge, pulling a heavy train over a steep mountain, it doesn't rely on strength, experience, or external validation. Instead, it repeats one simple phrase to itself: *"I think I can. I think I can."*

This mantra is a perfect illustration of how internal dialogue can shape our behavior and beliefs. The little engine isn't the biggest, fastest, or most qualified. But it keeps going, fueled by a belief in its own potential—something so many of us struggle with. In a world that often emphasizes outcomes, *The Little Engine That Could* reminds us that attitude and persistence matter just as much, if not more.

In the end, the engine makes it over the mountain not because it knew it could, but because it believed it could—long before it had proof. That's the magic of positive self-talk. It invites us to believe in ourselves before the world catches up.

Positive self-talk is more than feel-good fluff; it's a scientifically supported strategy for improving motivation, reducing stress, and enhancing performance. How we talk to ourselves—especially in moments of difficulty—directly impacts how we feel and how we act.

Positive Self-Talk: The Voice That Shapes Everything

At a young age, I realized that I had the power to determine whether the voice inside my head could be my friend or my enemy. Knowing that really became a superpower and allowed me to talk myself into a good place whenever needed. I had the unique experience early in my career to be given leadership roles very young. I often had staff much older than I was reporting to me, and stepped into situations where I had little to no experience. At times, my internal dialogue sounded a lot like doubt:

"Are you really ready for this?"

"What if you mess up?"

"Do you really belong here?"

These thoughts, left unchecked, become barriers to confidence and action. But fortunately, I would remember: **you can change the script.**

So, I intentionally replaced negative thoughts with supportive, encouraging ones. And it worked—especially under pressure. Jumping in to be my own cheerleader pushed me through unknowns and anxiety to get to the other side.

How I Use It as a Leader

Before a tough meeting, public talk, or big decision, I coach myself to calm my nervous system and quiet any unsupportive thoughts. You can create go-to phrases like:

- "I am capable of creating change."
- "My voice matters in this room."
- "I lead with purpose and compassion."

Or just be your own cheerleader and remind yourself that you can do it. Over time, these phrases become more than words—they become beliefs. They've helped me navigate self-doubt, anxiety, and specific challenges.

How You Can Start

1. **Catch your inner critic.** Get attuned to what you are telling yourself; you can even journal the negative thoughts that pop up.
2. **Flip the script.** Turn the chatter into affirming statements.
3. **Repeat positivity.** Say the positive self-talk quietly or out loud. Write down your positive statements. Keep them visible.
4. **Practice during stress.** Use them in real-time when you're nervous, tired, or facing a challenge.

Many say affirmations out loud in front of a mirror, but you can also just sit comfortably somewhere—your office, your car, or your living room and say them to yourself.

✍️ Write Your Own (some examples)

Area of Life	Affirmation
Confidence	"I trust myself to lead."
Purpose	"I am doing meaningful work."
Resilience	"I can handle challenges and grow from them."

Your Turn...what are your affirmations?

➡️   **Confidence:** _____

➡️   **Purpose:** _____

➡️   **Resilience:** _____

If the Little Engine can teach us to coach ourselves to success, we can look to another childhood "friend" who was instrumental in helping us see what we want to be—Harold, of *Harold and the Purple Crayon*. In this beloved children's book, Harold doesn't wait for the path to appear—he draws it himself. With nothing but a purple crayon and his imagination, he creates worlds, navigates challenges, and brings his vision to life one line at a time. Leading a mission-driven organization often feels the same. In a sector where resources are limited and roadmaps are rarely handed to you, **the ability to envision what doesn't yet exist**—a more equitable system, a funded initiative, a reimagined community—isn't a luxury; it's a necessity. Our ability to wake each day and envision a productive meeting, a successful speech, or a meaningful exchange with a donor is key to guiding ourselves to making it happen. Like Harold, I've learned that leadership begins with daring to draw the way forward, even when others can't yet see the picture.

Harold and the Purple Crayon may be a children's classic, but it holds profound lessons for leaders—especially those of us navigating uncharted territory in nonprofit work and social justice. Like Harold, leaders need to boldly embrace **vision**, creativity, and agency. Great leaders often have to see what isn't there yet—whether it's a more equitable community, a new program to serve those in need, or a solution to a systemic challenge. Like Harold, they must believe in their vision enough to begin drawing it themselves, even when the way forward is unclear.

Harold also reminds us that the path to success is rarely linear. He makes wrong turns, encounters obstacles, and sometimes gets lost—but he always draws his way forward again. That resilience and creative adaptability are vital traits for anyone leading change. The message is clear: **if you can envision it, you can begin to build it—one courageous stroke at a time.**

In a world that often demands certainty, *Harold and the Purple Crayon* invites readers to trust in their imagination, listen to their inner compass, and boldly co-create a better future.

Visualization: Seeing the Future Before It Happens

While positive self-talk rewires your *beliefs*, visualization helps you mentally rehearse your goals.

Before I walk into a high-stakes space—whether it's a funding pitch, a rally, or a conversation about policy—I *see* it first. I visualize the room, the conversation, my posture, and most importantly, the outcome that I want.

For me, seeing my desired outcome helps reinforce that it is possible and almost creates a "muscle memory" phenomenon that leads me down a familiar path back there.

How I Use Visualization as a Leader

A gala is an important event for a nonprofit like the YWCA Northern New Jersey. We rely on the evening to raise funds and friends to support our mission. The evening has many moving parts, from networking to award presentations to formal requests for money. With so much riding on me as the CEO to be a high performer for the evening, I always take time to include visualization as part of getting ready for the night. I intentionally imagine:

- ➡️ Walking into the venue with confidence and poise.
- ➡️ Engaging conversations with our attendees.
- ➡️ Speaking with conviction and compassion at the podium.

The result? I enter the gala not just prepared but grounded.

How to Start

Visualization doesn't take hours. Just 5–10 minutes to shift your mindset. Here's how:

1. **Choose a goal or event.** A meeting, an interview, a big decision.
2. **Close your eyes and imagine success.** Visualize the space, the people, your body language, and the conversation.
3. **Feel the emotions.** Confidence. Peace. Connection.
4. **Repeat.** The more you see it, the more natural it becomes.

Tip: Add this to your morning routine to imagine the kind of day you want to have or engage in it right before starting a major task.

⊚ Guided Visualization Template

Use this to guide your mental rehearsal:

♟ Find a quiet space. Close your eyes. Breathe deeply.

🎥 Imagine yourself walking into the space (meeting room, event, stage, office).

👑 Picture yourself standing tall, calm, and grounded.

💬 Hear yourself speaking clearly and confidently.

💘 Feel the energy of connection, purpose, and alignment.

🕊 Picture the outcome you want. Let it fill your body with belief.

➡ Set some Visualization Goals:

✦ BONUS PRACTICE: Mindset Check-In

Every week, reflect on the following:

Question	Your Answer
What does success look like today?	
What do I *need* to feel confident right now?	
How do I want to *show up* this week?	

Why This Inner Work Matters (Especially in Social Justice)

Leading social change is hard. You're often standing against deeply embedded systems, facing resistance, or carrying emotional burdens for your community. It's easy to burn out or doubt yourself.

Positive self-talk and visualization became my anchor points. They helped me.

- Stay grounded in values, not ego.
- Lead hard conversations with empathy.
- Bounce back from public and private setbacks.
- Stay connected to the *vision* of the world I'm working to build.

And I truly believe: if more changemakers prioritized this kind of mental and emotional fitness, we'd see even deeper, more sustainable progress.

Final Takeaway: Start With You

These practices will help you show up better. Remember:

- Your thoughts create your outcomes.
- Your inner voice sets the tone for your outward actions.
- You can lead with clarity—even in chaos—when you train your mind to focus and support you.

Start with just five minutes a day. One affirmation. One visualization. That's all it takes to begin the shift. Because when we strengthen our inner worlds, we become unstoppable in our outer ones.

Leaving you with one last children's book... one that I read to my children often when they were young—*Giraffes Can't Dance* by Giles Andreae. Gerald the giraffe is told he can't dance like the others. He feels out of place and awkward, but through patience, self-belief, imagining the steps he wants to take, and embracing his unique rhythm, Gerald finds his own way to shine, so remember:

- Practice self-compassion and affirm your worth daily.
- Envision your dance and choreograph your steps accordingly.

Leadership isn't about fitting into a mold—it's about creating your own dance that moves your mission forward. Like Gerald, when you embrace your unique rhythm, you can inspire real change both for yourself and others.

Remember —you are your greatest resource—and your mind is your most powerful tool!

LIVE IT!

Embrace the *moment*

We are all everyday changemakers – each of us contains the ability to make an impact in our own way.

What inspired Helen to be a changemaker?

AUTHOR'S REPLY:

Long before I stepped into boardrooms or taught college classes, my journey began on a simple school playground. I still remember that moment vividly—a classmate being bullied, isolated, afraid. I didn't know much back then, but I knew this: silence was not an option. So, I stood beside them. I offered support. I learned, in my own small way, the importance of showing up.

NOW IT IS YOUR TURN...

What inspires you to be a changemaker?

Helen invites you to reflect with two additional questions:

What are the messages you are telling yourself and how are they holding you back?

If you can only be what you see, what do you see for yourself and what needs to change in that vision so you can be the best version of yourself?

Visit the "Meet the Changemakers" section at the back of the book to connect with and learn more about all of the authors featured in **LIVE IT!**

CHAPTER 21

Listen
to Your Gut...
Even If You Don't Believe It

CHANGEMAKER: CHARLENE GORZELA

To my husband, Steve Zipper, who believes in me
and who helped me become a "We" and not just
a "Me," with some great laughs thrown in!

To my family, friends who are like family and those
who I've yet to meet – your presence, seen or unseen,
continues to shape and inspire me one day at a time.

"Your gut whispers the truth your heart already knows—trust it, and life becomes extraordinary."

– CHARLENE GORZELA

Trusting the Still, Small Voice Within That Knew Before I Did

People have always appreciated my optimistic outlook, welcoming spirit, and extroverted nature. But little did they know, there was a secret inner self behind the way I presented to the world—even from an early age.

In fall 2003, I was driving to work in Chicago, getting off the expressway ramp, listening to music, when a sudden wave of emotion overtook me. Out of nowhere, I began sobbing behind the wheel. It shocked me. What was there to cry about? Life was full and thriving on the outside. But inside, I felt trapped and misaligned in the fast-paced, people-intensive staffing firm I had owned since 1991.

Did I do anything about it? No. I shoved it down and bucked up.

Yet a small miracle followed. After some inner reflection, a voice within whispered: *"If you don't know your next step, maybe you're meant to stay where you are—for now."* That shift in perspective changed everything. I leaned into the uncertainty, dove deeper into my business and life, and chose trust. Not because I had it all figured out—far from it—but because I believed that more would be revealed.

Running and owning a business has a lot of moving parts. I operated on a wing, a prayer, and a one-day-at-a-time attitude. The most important belief I held was that my company—and everyone in it—was part of my life legacy. That belief carried me through challenges, wins, surprises, and moments of doubt. My gut, my intuition—that still, small voice—was the compass I returned to when fear or hopelessness crept in.

The Apartment Below the Earth

In the early 1980s, I lived in what I called "the apartment below the earth," a garden-level studio in Chicago. It was small, often dark and dingy, but it was mine. Dinner was ramen noodles or takeout chicken. I worked retail on Michigan Avenue, dusting figurines in a collectibles store. With only a high school diploma and no clear direction, I wasn't dreaming big. I was partying—drinking, staying up late, numbing.

Underneath the laughter and wild nights was a quiet desperation I couldn't name. I remember smoking my first joint in seventh or eighth grade, then sitting in my Catholic school uniform the next morning, terrified someone would smell it on me. My gut didn't say, "Stop." It said nothing. Or maybe I just stopped listening.

The Sobriety I Didn't See Coming

By 1988, my life was a series of late nights, blurred mornings, and emotional fog. I thought I was just a party girl. I didn't realize I was self-medicating to avoid pain I couldn't face.

I'd thought about seeing a psychiatrist once. I asked my mom. Her response: "You're strong. You don't need that." It came from her own family beliefs—we don't share too much. People might use it against you. That ended the conversation.

Eventually, life forced me to wake up. After a stormy night out and a canceled coffee date with an old friend who'd gotten sober, I called him the next morning to apologize. Instead, I blurted out, *"How did you stop drinking?"* Before the call, my head said no. But my heart and my gut said yes.

He picked me up and took me to Northwestern Hospital for an evaluation. The therapist recommended outpatient treatment. And in that moment, I had a flash of clarity. Fear wrapped around me like a cloak. I was afraid to drink and afraid not to. But the jig was up. Something had to change.

It was a gut punch unlike anything I'd felt. But that pain became my turning point. I had no idea what lay ahead, only that I had to stop. And I did.

Getting sober wasn't one big decision. It was hundreds of tiny ones. Quiet, courageous choices made hour by hour. That intuitive hit, that voice within, saved me.

To Thine Own Self Be True — William Shakespeare

As a born optimist and a future entrepreneur in the making, I always tried to put a positive spin on everything. But optimism without truth had a cost. I talked a big game but didn't know how to execute my ideas. I settled for mediocrity, until I finally surrendered—not just to sobriety, but to a new way of living.

Pushed by pain, I became pulled by a vision. I needed Life 101 at thirty years old. I had to stop living by my wits and start doing the next right thing. I didn't know everything, and for the first time, that was okay. The fog lifted. The sky seemed bluer, the trees greener, the world more vibrant.

At work, things clicked. I was a recruiter, and I earned more that month in outpatient treatment than I had in months prior. I showed up differently, more focused, more alive. As part of my healing, a mentor asked me to give her a daily "weather report"—sunny, cloudy, stormy—to help me recognize my feelings. It was simple, and it worked.

And the Beat of Life Goes On...

For years, I didn't believe in magic, but something inside me did. A whisper that said, *There's more.* More happiness. More purpose. More me.

That's the beauty of intuition. It doesn't need you to be ready. It just needs you to be willing.

For a long time, I wasn't. I ignored the discomfort, the misalignment. I stayed in relationships I knew weren't right. I married someone despite gut-level doubts and divorced him a year later. I lost jobs. I wore the mask of "I've got this" while quietly unraveling.

What kept me from listening? My saboteurs—those mental voices I didn't yet have names for. My Judge told me I was dumb. The Avoider helped me ignore red flags. The Hyper-Achiever insisted I could outwork the ache inside. The Pleaser begged me to win people over before I loved myself. And the Controller tried to hold it all together.

The biggest lie I believed? That those voices were smarter than me. Eventually, the pain of not listening became greater than the fear of change. That's when the real journey began.

The Gut, the Heart, and the Mind — The Sacred Sequence of Trust

Today, my gut, heart, and mind work in unison. That's how I know it's a true yes.

For me, it starts with the gut—a knowing, a flash of clarity without explanation. It doesn't shout. It nudges.

Gut: *Something's not right. Something has to change.*

Heart: *I want something better. I want to feel whole.*

Mind: *Here's how we'll do it.*

If I had gone to my mind first, I never would have moved. If I had stayed only in my gut, I would've remained stuck in fear. But together—the gut, the heart, the mind—they became a lifeline.

I stopped living by my surface mind, the survival part of my brain. That's where saboteurs live. I'd nurtured those voices for so long without realizing it. I'd learned to survive, but not to thrive. When I shifted into the part of my brain that responds with positivity and purpose, clarity arrived in ways I'd never imagined.

Fast Forward: Saying Yes Without Logic

In my early twenties, I said yes to a recruiter job in downtown Chicago. No experience, no plan, 100 percent commission. People said, "Get a real job." I followed my gut instead.

Years later, I acquired a small staffing agency. Because of a soft business climate, I was able to acquire, by miracle, a small unsecured loan from a friend who, for some crazy reason, believed in me. I owned it for twenty-six years. It wasn't easy managing people, culture, client demands, and my own growth all at once. I wore many hats, held people through their challenges, and learned to build trust from the inside out. What made it magical wasn't just the placements or revenue; it was the lives we touched, the confidence we helped rebuild, and the belief we restored in people's ability to grow and succeed.

Eventually, I realized I wasn't meant to be the day-to-day president anymore. My gifts were evolving. I wanted to return to my creative, entrepreneurial roots—and I did. I moved to Los Angeles and transitioned into a CEO role. One of the women I'd hired—bright, talented, driven—ended up buying the company twelve years later. A true win-win. If I had written out a plan, I would've sold myself short. That was the power of listening to something deeper.

During those twenty-six years, I also began studying human potential—discovering how to know myself as a whole person, get vulnerable, take risks, and believe that every challenge holds a hidden gift. That career became my training ground not only professionally, but also personally and spiritually.

I learned to Explore, to show Empathy, to Innovate, Navigate, and Activate—even when I was scared. I now guide others through reinvention and self-trust. I help people access the pure potentiality within them that makes their hearts soar in life and in business.

A therapist once told me, when I expressed frustration about my ex-husband not living up to his potential: *"Charlene, potential has a shelf life."* That hit me. I had ignored my doubts when I got married. I didn't listen to my gut—again. But I learned from it. That marriage ended, and it taught me invaluable lessons. It also taught me that my potential had a shelf life unless I made a break from some of my decisions.

Today, I'm married to a man I had zero doubts about. I followed my intuition, even though he wasn't the "type" I thought I needed. But our core values aligned, and my heart—backed by wisdom—said yes. My first marriage was a "me." This one is a "we." And that makes all the difference.

Putting It All Together: Mental Fitness + Cellular Activation

Today, the work I do with others is rooted in the connection between mental fitness and cellular vitality. Why? Because how we think and how our bodies function are deeply intertwined.

Mental fitness isn't about thinking positively all the time. It's about learning to shift from our sabotaging, survival mind (left brain) to our creative, wise, and calm inner mind (right brain). The left brain is where the Judge, Pleaser, Controller, and other destructive mental habits live. The right brain is home to empathy, clarity, creativity, and deep insight. Through practice, people can recognize their mental habits and build new neural pathways that allow them to respond to life with happiness, resilience, and purpose.

And the body? It matters too. When we support our bodies at the *cellular level*—reducing oxidative stress, balancing hormones, enhancing energy—our mind gets clearer. Our nervous system calms. Our moods stabilize. I believe in helping people activate their body's own intelligence, not just treat symptoms. That's where true vitality and longevity come in.

For me, sobriety gave me the doorway to rediscover all of this. The inner voice that saved my life continues to guide my work. When people come to me for support, whether it's in shifting their business, healing from burnout, or simply finding joy again, I don't offer a one-size-fits-all plan. I help them listen. To their gut, heart, and mind. Because inside every person is a still, small voice that already knows the way.

And when we trust it, our lives begin to unfold in ways better than we could have ever imagined for us individually and the world.

LIVE IT!

Embrace the *moment*

We are all everyday changemakers – each of us contains the ability to make an impact in our own way.

What inspired Charlene to be a changemaker?

AUTHOR'S REPLY:

When I work with clients—whether personally or in a leadership role—I feel like I'm part of their team. I help them bring out the wisdom already within. When they feel there's no way out, I help them discover there's always a way. And when they remember the power of who they really are—that's everything to me and hopefully them.

NOW IT IS YOUR TURN...

What inspires you to be a changemaker?

Charlene invites you to reflect with two additional questions:

What is a quiet nudge that could be nudging you just recently, or a nudge that has popped up throughout the years that you have ignored and judged as "bad"? How does it feel when you ignore it?

If you had no outside obligations in your life, what would you change, either big or small?

Visit the "Meet the Changemakers" section at the back of the book to connect with and learn more about all of the authors featured in **LIVE IT!**

CHAPTER 22

A Smile.
A Helping Hand.
A Dance in the Street.

CHANGEMAKER: TERESE RÖLKE

To my parents, who showed me the strength of
kindness, compassion, and determination.

To my husband, for his unwavering love, support,
and partnership.

To my son, whose devotion to following a spiritual path
different from how he was raised inspires me every day.

This is for all who dare to live with heart, lead with love,
and leave the world a little better than they found it.

"Everything happens in its perfect way, whether
we realize it or not at the time. Challenges, setbacks,
and even moments of uncertainty are part of a
greater process — one that shapes us into who
we're meant to be."

– TERESE RÖLKE

*G*rowing up in Brooklyn gave me character. It made me strong and determined. I believed I could do anything if I put my heart into it.

My mother was the kindest person I knew. Everyone loved her. I wanted to be just like her. I enjoyed helping Mom with housework—from doing laundry to vacuuming. She had a full-time job at Midwood High School and went back to school at night to further her education.

When I was eleven or twelve, Mom would leave me instructions on how to cook dinner for our family of four whenever she was out. I loved being the little mama who took care of our family for Mom.

Dad enjoyed sports and was handy around the house. We had no boys in our family, so Dad taught me how to hit a softball and throw and catch a football. When he wanted to take out a window in the kitchen, he taught me how to lay bricks to close the hole.

When I was about fifteen or sixteen, Dad put a painter's hat on my head, a mask over my nose and mouth, and gave me a crowbar. He told me to knock down the walls of the small bathroom in the kitchen. I had a blast! After we cleaned up the mess, I helped him put up the sheetrock and tiles. Of course, I corrected him when he didn't follow the tile patterns!

Throughout my life, Dad called me "My Daughter, My Son." I was honored by this title, which he called me right up until he passed away in 2024.

Determination to Start My Career

In my last semester before I graduated from Brooklyn College with a TV/Radio degree, I was determined to find one final internship that could potentially become a full-time career. I saw that American Express in New York City was on the list, so I called. I was told that they no longer had an internship program. I asked them to honor the fact that they were still on our list and let me come in for an interview—then they could take themselves off the list for the next semester. They agreed. I got the internship!

The chairman of the TV/Radio Department at Brooklyn College told us not to expect our internships to turn into full-time jobs because the field is competitive. I felt that if I made myself valuable during my internship and developed meaningful relationships, they would want me to stay. I was right! Once my internship was finished, they paid me as a per diem freelancer for three months until they created a staff position for me.

Giving Back

Years into my career doing corporate video production work for American Express, I suggested that we restart the internship program. I felt that we could help college students get the real-world experience they needed while training them to become potential per diem freelancers for us to hire when they graduated. This was a win-win situation for the interns and us!

I was proud and honored to implement and oversee our new internship program. It was a full-circle moment! The feedback I received from our interns later in their careers was incredible. They gave credit to our internship program and freelance work for launching their careers!

For years, American Express supported "Take Our Daughters to Work Day." For our department, Creative Media, to be included in the initiative and to give the girls a fun, unique, and memorable experience, I created a short "news" program that enabled them to work with our professional video crew in our studio and control room.

They operated cameras, the teleprompter, audio, and lights. They got to be the on-camera news anchors reading the teleprompter. They stood in the control room and watched the technical director cut the live show. They hit the record button to capture the program on video.

After that, we had them meet and talk with our graphic designers, who worked on creating print media. Then they met and talked with our management staff. At the end of the day, they all received a video copy of the brief news program we created. I was happy when their experience with us was rated at the top of the surveys every year!

Getting Married and Moving to New Jersey

My husband and I were the pioneers in the family. When we got married, we were the first to leave Brooklyn and move to Central New Jersey. We planted our flag in Monmouth

County, drawn by its beautiful parks and beaches—a perfect place to raise a family.

Never Doubt the Child... Learn from Them

The best experience in the world is raising a child. They begin life with a clean slate, full of potential and promise. As parents, it's our responsibility—and privilege—to provide them with positive experiences, to teach, guide, and direct them, all while giving them the freedom to discover who they truly are.

If we are open to listening, we discover that the learning is mutual. They view the world through a lens of curiosity and honesty, unfiltered by years of learned behavior. Their fresh perspective often reminds us of what really matters.

Children are naturally intuitive. They can sense when something isn't right, when someone is hurting, or when joy is genuine. When we allow them space to express themselves freely, they surprise us with their insight, compassion, and creativity.

Serving with Purpose

I thrive on making a positive difference in the lives of others. My journey in volunteerism began as a Cub Scout Leader for five years—an experience that allowed me to help shape young minds through teamwork, leadership, and outdoor adventures.

I also served in my son's school as vice president and president of the PTO. One of my greatest joys was creating events that brought parents, teachers, and children together—moments filled with fun, laughter, and connection that helped strengthen the school community.

Over the years, I've continued to serve in a wide variety of volunteer roles throughout the community—wherever I saw a need, I did my best to step in and help.

In April 2013, I had the privilege of meeting Orly Wahba, the founder of Life Vest Inside, at the Monmouth County Chamber of Commerce's Women in Business Luncheon. Her mission to promote worldwide kindness instantly resonated with me. I approached her after the event and said, "I've lived my life focused on kindness! How can I help?"

That one question changed my path.

I became a Life Vest Inside Ambassador and the New Jersey Group Leader for the annual Worldwide Dance for Kindness for the next seven years. What began as a small gathering of just sixty people dancing on the boardwalk in Pier Village, Long Branch, grew into a vibrant, joy-filled celebration with over 200 people dancing on Broad Street in Red Bank.

The event quickly became a beloved community tradition. The Navesink Hook & Ladder Company proudly set up Fire Truck No. 1, flying the American flag from the top of the ladder while firefighters danced with us. Local dance studios joined in, teaching children and their families the choreography each year and helping to spread the message of unity through movement.

A Girl Scout Troop became part of our tradition as well, bringing energy and enthusiasm each year. Grace Christian Church in Tinton Falls generously donated sidewalk chalk, allowing children to decorate Broad Street with colorful messages of kindness that remained visible for days—a beautiful, lingering reminder of what we stood for.

The impact this had on the community was both positive and powerful. We created not just an event, but lasting memories and connections that reminded people of the good we're all capable of when we come together with love, purpose, and a little dancing in the street.

Continuing the Spirit of Kindness

Looking back, I'm incredibly proud of the joy, unity, and love we sparked through something as simple—and as powerful—as kindness. What started as a desire to make a difference became a movement that brought people of all ages, backgrounds, and walks of life together with one shared purpose: to be kind and to inspire others to do the same.

Kindness is contagious. It doesn't cost anything, yet it can change everything. Whether it's through a smile, a helping hand, a dance in the street, or a chalk-drawn message left behind for a stranger, every act of kindness leaves a mark.

I believe we all have the ability—and the responsibility—to make a positive difference in the world around us. It doesn't take grand gestures. It takes heart, consistency, and the willingness to say, "How can I help?"

That's where the magic begins.

Volunteering for the Chamber

During the years I volunteered with Life Vest Inside, I also cultivated meaningful relationships through my involvement with the Monmouth County Chamber, which later became the Monmouth Regional Chamber of Commerce.

When I was a new member, I noticed the executive director was handling credit card payments at our weekly "Perkolator" breakfast meetings. Wanting to help, I asked him to show me how to take over the process so he could focus on greeting and speaking with members and potential members.

That simple act opened the door for something greater. I genuinely enjoyed welcoming everyone as they arrived each week, and I soon expanded that role to other chamber events. Being helpful and informative came naturally—I loved answering questions and supporting attendees with anything they needed.

A few years into my membership, I was humbled and honored when the chamber president informed me that the board of directors had voted to bring me on as a new board member. As part of the role, each board member is responsible for chairing a committee, and I didn't hesitate to request the Membership Committee. Supporting our members and promoting the chamber to new people aligned perfectly with my passion for connection and community.

After serving as a board member for a few years, another opportunity presented itself. The executive director position became available. I threw my hat in the ring. I was passionate about volunteering for the chamber, so I figured I could have a greater impact by leading the chamber! My position as the executive director started in December 2019.

I love making connections for our members and collaborating with them. Creating events for them to expand their networks, learn, and be inspired. Giving them the support and opportunities they need to thrive!

As Mark Twain said, "Choose a job you love, and you will never have to work a day in your life!"

Unconditional Love…and an Unconventional Path

A mother's love for her son runs deep. It's a bond that is unconditional, unwavering, and eternal.

As parents, we all hope and pray that our children grow into lives filled with purpose, happiness, and authenticity. We dream about their future—envisioning paths we think will bring them joy, success, and belonging. But as they grow, we come to understand an important truth: their journey is theirs alone.

Sometimes, the road our children choose doesn't look like the one we imagined. It may be unexpected, unconventional, or unfamiliar. But it's ours to support, not shape.

Flexibility, acceptance, and open-hearted listening are some of the greatest gifts we can offer our children. We must be willing to grow with them, to expand our own perspectives, and to love them not in spite of their choices—but because of who they authentically are and what they believe in.

Watching my son step into his own light—even if it took time or came in unexpected ways—filled me with a kind of pride that comes from seeing your child embrace their truth, regardless of what the world thinks. That kind of courage is rare and beautiful.

Yes, the path may be unconventional. But it is rich with meaning, shaped by integrity, and rooted in love. And as his mother, there is nothing more important to me than knowing he has found his purpose. He is a true Devotee.

A Life of Purpose

Each chapter of my life has been guided by the same simple principle: lead with kindness, act with purpose, and give where you can.

Whether it was helping a college intern find their footing, creating a joyful moment for a child, supporting a fellow chamber member, or dancing in the streets to celebrate compassion—I've always believed that one person can, and does, make a difference.

I will continue to show up, lift others, and share kindness wherever I go. That, to me, is a life well lived.

We are all everyday changemakers - each of us has the ability to make an impact in our own way.

LIVE IT!

Embrace the *moment*

We are all everyday changemakers – each of us contains the ability to make an impact in our own way.

What inspired Terese to be a changemaker?

AUTHOR'S REPLY:

Collaboration helps us lift each other up — because we are stronger together. Being a changemaker isn't about working alone; it's about service, compassion, and building something better for everyone. When we unite around shared values and common goals, real change becomes possible. I believe that by supporting one another, we can create a world where everyone has the opportunity to thrive.

NOW IT IS YOUR TURN...

What inspires you to be a changemaker?

Terese invites you to reflect with two additional questions:

What moments or experiences from your own upbringing have shaped your sense of purpose, and how are you using them to impact others today?

When someone looks back on your life, what do you hope they'll say was the difference you made—and are you living in alignment with that hope right now?

Visit the "Meet the Changemakers" section at the back of the book to connect with and learn more about all of the authors featured in **LIVE IT!**

CHAPTER 23

The Gift in the Wreckage: How My Mess Became My *Mission*

CHANGEMAKER: TANYA NEWBOULD

My daughter, Ava, for being the evolution in my life
that leads to a legacy for others.

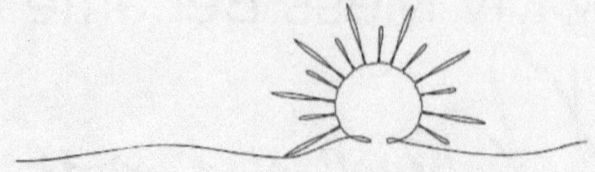

"I want you to know your pain and trauma do
not discount you. It creates a sacred space of
understanding, enabling you to cultivate compassion
and resilience to change the world. Never, ever give up,
the time is now!"

– TANYA NEWBOULD

*H*ave you ever thought, "It's over?" You look at your life and think, "I've suffered through trauma," "I have nothing to give," or "the best part of my life is over, ruined." What if I were to tell you the best is yet to come? What if, even at the age of ninety, you may have a contribution that could be the most significant act in your life? What if you were to witness or be a part of a miracle beyond your wildest dreams? What if you experience a trauma that you think is the worst thing that could happen, only to learn that it is your gift in the wreckage?

This is my story.

"I think I want a baby!" James exclaimed with a smile on his face and a twinkle in his light green eyes. "You want a baby now? But I'm forty; you said you didn't want children," I replied in disbelief. "Well, I've been thinking about it, and I wasn't ready before; I think I am now."

Typically, this conversation would occur much earlier in a marriage. We had been married for eleven years, and my gorgeous husband is seven and a half years younger than I am, which put him at a ripe thirty-four. "Okay... wow... I mean, awesome." As he continued, his wavy brown hair hanging in his face, I tuned into the birds chirping outside the kitchen window in a nearby tree, like Snow White in a Disney setting. This is what I've wanted to hear for years. I'm adopted and have longed for a genuine bloodline connection. But at forty, I had settled into the fact that being an actor and having fur babies would be my life. Six years ago, he didn't want children, and being that I married the right GUY for me, what was I to do? Leave the man of my dreams to find a dude to father my child, or accept the reality and find a new sense of purpose and happiness? I chose the latter.

The good news, if you can call it that, is that I didn't realize your chances of getting pregnant go down significantly after thirty-five, and once you're forty, it drops to less than a 10% chance of a natural conception. I sometimes think that because I didn't have this knowledge, I simply didn't worry about it and assumed I would get pregnant easily. Whatever you focus on, you create more of it, and I believed that it would happen *eventually*. We began trying, and it was fun; we were excited. Month after month, we would try, but month after month, it didn't come to fruition. The joy slowly morphed into sadness, but I held high hopes that I would one day have my baby. Two years flew by, and I still wasn't pregnant.

I sat down quietly in my bedroom and closed my eyes. There was heaviness in my heart. A familiar feeling I had known since birth, one that confirmed, "You don't get to have it all; you don't deserve it." I didn't know what to do, so I prayed, "God, this isn't happening, so if you want me to have a baby, you're going to have to make it happen because it's not. Please God, please, hear my prayer."

Three months later, my prayer was answered when I missed my period and thought it was jet lag from our trip to Thailand. Let's say "One Night in Bangkok" isn't just a song! Maybe I do deserve this blessing. It's going to be perfect because I will have a proper blood connection to love that I've never known, I thought.

I had a healthy pregnancy, but at four and a half months, I found myself on my gray slate kitchen floor, crying so hard that snot was dripping from my nose and drool from my mouth. "Dorothy, I don't think we're in Kansas anymore."

I began therapy to try to understand what was going on. I didn't know I was suffering from antenatal depression, one of nine levels of Perinatal Mood & Anxiety Disorders (PMADs).

I scheduled a C-Section. I was forty-three, and I didn't want to take any chances of losing this blessing that I was deemed to have. The morning arrived when our little girl was to be born. I was nervous, yet excited. I loved carrying her in my belly; now I will get to hold her, love her, and have the connection I had always craved.

The epidural worked, and the operation went smoothly. I held my breath until I heard her cry. She sounded like a baby kitten. James followed our baby, and I went into recovery. I spent the next six hours violently shaking and throwing up. This traumatic birthing recovery was the beginning of seven out of nine PMADs.

For the next five and a half months, I thought my life was over; it was done. I suffered in silence. I was a horrible human being who didn't know how to connect to my baby. I knew I loved her, but I couldn't connect to the motherly feelings everyone talked about. Instead, I thought I was crazy, horrible, a monster that had ruined my baby's life, my marriage, and my life as I knew it.

My friends were scared for me; they had never witnessed me behaving the way I was, and my best friend, Danielle, took me to breakfast one morning and broke down, "Something's wrong with you." "I'm tired, I had a baby!" I retorted. "No, this is different," she spoke through her tears. This terrified me because I knew she was right.

I refused to take antidepressants, although now I coach people to do so if needed. I was diagnosed with postpartum depression, anxiety, PTSD, obtrusive thoughts, and panic disorder. I sought recovery through 5-HTP and Rose Hip Oil. Two weeks later, I stepped out of my darkness into the light and could finally embrace the motherhood I had craved. What I couldn't embrace was that I could hardly find any information on postpartum depression.

I was interviewed for a documentary about actors called "Die Trying," directed by another new mom, Jamielyn Lippman. She was strong and knew her stuff. I had been thinking about the lack of information and said to her, "I have an idea for a documentary about postpartum depression, and I want you to direct it." She paused and said, "I didn't have it, I'm sorry." She registered my look of disappointment. "I'll tell you what, I'll put a post on a mommy site, and if anyone responds, I'll let you know." With a grateful smile on my face, I thanked her.

Twenty-four hours later, she called me with excitement in her voice. "I think you're right; we've had over 100 responses from women saying they would give their testimony. Let's meet."

As the journey progressed and we gathered testimonies, doctors' insights, cultural differences, and learned about the lack of information available for maternal mental health, our awareness grew, and so did my passion for these women.

Devastation set in when we lost two of our amazing women to suicide two weeks apart, shortly after we had finished filming. I was at Disneyland when I received the second phone call. My daughter looked up at me from her stroller, registering my emotions. "Mama, what's wrong?" I couldn't speak. Everything was moving in slow motion as I stared at the Disney castle.

I couldn't fall apart. I still had the rest of the day to spend with her. The moment hit me when I hoisted her onto my hip. "Mama, I know you're sad; it's okay, I'm here for you, and I love you." She took my face in her tiny hands and kissed me gently. I couldn't stop the tears from coming, but that didn't seem to bother her. We hugged each other tight and watched the beautiful fireworks adorning the sky.

What I realized at that moment is that the love and connection I craved by having a baby were always with me from the moment she was conceived. I have been blessed with a beautiful daughter; the love she shows me daily is the greatest gift I have ever received. I am not alone, I am not abandoned, I am loved, and I am truly blessed.

Over the next eight years, with the help of our other creator, Lindsay Gerszt, and Executive Producer, and narrator Brooke Shields, "When the Bough Breaks—a documentary about Postpartum Depression" was released. It has been viewed in over sixty countries and six languages, and viewed on Netflix for a year and a half. It has saved lives and families.

On March 14, 2020, the world shut down due to the COVID-19 pandemic. This left me with a similar feeling of postpartum depression, and equally as scary. The feeling that life as I knew it was over, done, and there were thoughts of everyone dying. This level of fear is indeed beyond what most people experience, but it also leads to seeking solutions, taking action, and enduring extreme mental discomfort.

As I settled into this understanding, despite a tremendous loss of life and connection, my inquiry became: how can I serve people, how can I make a difference beyond myself, and my own family?

People often came to me for advice, whether it be on a relationship, starting a new business, postpartum depression, or motherhood in general. Zoom had become the new way to communicate and stay connected while we weren't allowed to gather. I decided to see if I could help people by coaching a select few beta clients. The feedback was "Keep going."

In 2021, I became certified with Advanced Certification in PMADs from Postpartum Support International. By 2023, I had acquired my ACC (Associate Certified Coach) credential, as well as my global ICF (International Coach Federation) credentials. In 2024, I became a LAT (Licensed Academy Trainer) for the Academy for Coaching Excellence, and I recently received my Trauma-Informed Coaching certification from the Voyage Academy of London in 2025.

Due to these credentials, I serve as a keynote speaker with passion and purpose. I coach individuals, businesses, and corporations to see their true magnificence, transforming their world and, therefore, the world around them.

I didn't want to take medications when I was suffering from depression and anxiety, so I was always searching for ways to ground myself. In 2018, my beloved mom passed away in only five days from a combination of heart failure and the discovery of tumors in her lungs. The night before she went to meet God, I stayed with her in her hospital room. Riddled with anxiety and exhaustion from the previous days, I was offered a sleeping pill. I declined because I knew time was precious, and I chose to be present. The nurse gave me cotton balls filled with lavender, and it worked. It calmed me enough for me to sleep for several hours. At 8:05 p.m., my mom took her last breath, and I witnessed her being born into her spirit life (that's another book).

Lighting Up Life in Another Way

In 2022, I was asked to collaborate on my own candle line. My theme was to create a sense of grounding that helps individuals find a way to feel centered and calm, beyond relying on medication. SOZO Heart candles, diffusers, and roller oils were born. SOZO is a Greek word meaning restoration of one's being, encompassing physical, mental, and spiritual well-being. I now have a distributor, and the brand is experiencing rapid growth in spas, resorts, and retail locations. This ties into the message of my brand: to create change, make a difference, and create a sense of "All is Well".

I share this not to impress you, but to impress upon you that in the wreckage of each of our lives, there are tremendous gifts, and what you may think is your MESS may become YOUR message. CHOOSE not to be a victim. CHOOSE to make a difference.

If I can do it, you can too, the time is now!

LIVE IT!

Embrace the *moment*

We are all everyday changemakers – each of us contains the ability to make an impact in our own way.

What inspired Tanya to be a changemaker?

AUTHOR'S REPLY:

I know what it feels like to be cracked open by life—to stand in the wreckage and wonder if I'll ever feel whole again. That pain, that breaking - gave me more than scars; it gave me a voice. I became a changemaker because I refused to let my suffering be silent. I wanted to offer other women what I once needed: truth without shame, support without judgment, and the reminder that healing is not just possible—it's profound. I'm inspired by the women who show up anyway—the ones juggling everything, carrying invisible weight, and still choosing to rise. I do this work because if I can be a mirror that reflects someone's worth back to them, if I can turn my wounds into a map for someone else's holistic healing, then none of it will have been wasted. Change doesn't always start with a megaphone. Sometimes, it begins with a whisper, a conversation, a candle lit in the dark. That's the change I'm here to make.

NOW IT IS YOUR TURN...

What inspires you to be a changemaker?

Tanya invites you to reflect with two additional questions:

What has happened in your life that you question "Why did that happen to me?" Instead ask "Why is this happening for me?"

What do you not want to look at within you? Whatever you are avoiding has control over your life. Choose to look, see, tell the truth and take authentic action. Your mess will also be your mission

Visit the "Meet the Changemakers" section at the back of the book to connect with and learn more about all of the authors featured in **LIVE IT!**

CHAPTER 24

Be Accountable for Your Life... The Journey is Guided by Your

Choices

CHANGEMAKER: NICHOLAS MARCO

Dedicated to my dad, John Marco

"Vulnerability has been my greatest teacher,
and opportunity its favorite student."

– NICHOLAS MARCO

*E*very human being is given just one opportunity to live their life. There is no rewind button, no fast-forward button, and there's certainly no pause. Time is a one-way street. Every second that passes is gone forever, never to return. That realization used to terrify me, because for so much of my early life, I was not truly living. I was simply surviving inside a version of myself that wasn't authentic.

For me, the first two decades of life weren't lived with intention, but in constant reaction; reacting to expectations, to my own restless mind, and to feelings I didn't know how to process. My childhood was marked by contradictions. At school, I was the high achiever the teachers loved, and I was the one whose report cards glowed with praise. At home, I was moody, restless, and often defiant, and that grew especially toward the two people who loved me most, my parents. They gave me unconditional love, but I gave them constant frustration. To my teachers, I looked like I had it all figured out. The truth was, I felt like I was quietly unraveling. On the outside, I looked like the kid with the answers. However, on the inside, I felt like a fraud sitting at a desk waiting to be exposed.

Later in life, I would learn my behavioral challenges in adolescence were caused by having both ADHD and OCD, and I waited some twenty-plus years to be diagnosed. Even before I knew the words for it, I felt the weight of those conditions every day. The restlessness, the obsession with details, and the inability to quiet my mind all combined into an exhausting internal storm.

If that weren't enough, I carried a shadow of major depression that followed me everywhere. It was a darkness no one could see, but I felt it pressing down on me constantly. I was battling with a significant part of my identity: my sexuality. I was attracted to men, not women, and I prayed every night that the feeling would disappear. I begged God to change me, believing that if I could just wake up "normal," the torment would end. The idea of saying out loud that I was gay was simply unfathomable. To me, it wasn't just a secret; it was a source of shame I couldn't imagine surviving if anyone knew.

My actions were shaped by a constant fear of judgment, and stepping outside social norms simply didn't feel like an option. I lived with tunnel vision. I couldn't glance to the left and enjoy what was happening "over there," nor could I look to the right, as any deviation might be perceived as "not normal." The only path that felt safe was the straight and narrow. Doing something fully authentic to myself seemed like an unattainable dream. I drifted through life like a clenched fist, releasing the pressure only when I was alone, hiding my vulnerabilities so no one could see them. The trouble was, time kept slipping by, and with every year that passed, the awareness of it grew sharper. Looking back, I see that the journey could have been so much more fulfilling and joyful, but in those moments, I simply had no idea.

While my inner world felt restricted, life around me kept moving forward. My father was entering the boldest chapter of his own life, launching what would become an international brand. At forty-nine, he founded what is now

Hand & Stone Massage and Facial Spa. I was fortunate to work in his first location, in my hometown. Working the front desk as a shy, awkward, introverted kid would later prove invaluable to shaping my communication skills and teaching me how to connect with people. By the time I graduated from high school, I ranked number two in my class and had the honor of speaking at commencement. On paper, I was ready to embark on the path to becoming a doctor. From the outside, everything appeared to be falling perfectly into place. Yet beneath that polished surface, I was adrift. I didn't have clarity about what I truly wanted, and I was deeply disconnected from any real sense of happiness. It was as if I was following a script that had been written for me; don't dare question whether it was the right one, just follow along to blend in.

Fast forward to the second half of my college years, when my strength to stay guarded finally began to weaken. I came out. My heart raced, my palms were sweating, and for a moment I thought the words might choke me before they ever left my lips. But somehow, I pushed them out. I was met with an outpouring of love and support from so many friends and family members that I legitimately felt like I was born again. When this incredibly heavy weight was finally removed from my chest, the tunnel vision vanished. Suddenly, I wasn't on autopilot anymore—I was behind the wheel. I could drive anywhere and be anyone. Each day, my love for myself grew, and I had the confidence to be unapologetically me, caring less about the judgment of others. I was free. I saw that the possibilities for how I spend my seconds are limitless. It hit me: I am the biggest influence on my life's direction. My influence, through my choices, is much more significant than that of my environment or that of other people. I am in control, but for so long, I was not taking control. I needed to experience discomfort through vulnerability to grow.

I graduated from Penn State University with a B.S. in Biochemistry and Molecular Biology. Did I enjoy the subject? Yes. Did I love it? No. I chose it for one reason: it had the highest acceptance rate into medical school. It was the "smart" choice, the "safe" choice. But it was never truly mine. As graduation approached, I never even took the MCAT. Deep down, I knew my hesitation meant something—I wasn't on the right path.

On graduation day, sitting among my peers in the school of science, I felt out of place. How had I made it through four years of sleepless nights without a clear direction? Yet in that uncertainty, I felt something new: empowerment. For the first time, I wasn't blindly following a script. I was free to write my own.

My next move felt so shocking to me, but it was so logical; I enrolled in nursing school. When shadowing doctors during undergrad, I discovered the nurse anesthetist career. It was a more advanced nursing degree that required a lot of knowledge and skill, but it also came with a nice work-life balance and high compensation. The old me would have felt guilty for considering things like work-life balance and pay over the astuteness of being a medical doctor. Nursing became my fresh start, my chance to enter a space that felt aligned with who I was becoming. From day one, I showed up as myself—authentic, energized, reborn. Nick Marco 2.0. People noticed. My energy had shifted, and before long, I was elected class president. For the first time, I wasn't just checking boxes; I was thriving.

Along the way, I worked as a patient care technician in a local hospital to gain experience. That job lit something inside me—I felt alive, connected, purposeful. My experience paid off, and after graduation, I landed my first position in the ICU. It was a milestone I had worked toward tirelessly, and for a moment, I felt unstoppable.

One day, my father called to let me know that the development of a brand-new Hand & Stone location had become available, and something inside me immediately said, "Go for it." I believed in the brand, in my father's vision, and in the positive impact it had on people, so I jumped at the opportunity, knowing I would have the support of my sister, who was going to be heavily involved. The same week I began my job in the ICU, my first Hand & Stone location opened. In the final month of grand opening preparation, my sister went on bed rest, pregnant with twins. My first year as a nurse was already intense, but that intensity was magnified tenfold by the parallel challenge of being a business owner. Juggling the demands of patient care and entrepreneurship tested every ounce of my energy, patience, and resilience.

Despite the pressure, the business flourished in its first year. From the outside, everything looked like a success. But inside, doubts crept in. My natural tendency to worry about disappointing others made leadership feel heavy and, at times, isolating. As my drive to grow my business portfolio grew, I wrestled with guilt about leaving nursing. Ultimately, I knew I had to choose my sanity. Resigning from nursing was one of the hardest decisions I ever made, yet I understood that my full energy and dedication needed to go into Hand & Stone. This was my calling.

As we grew, I discovered that the more challenges I took on, the more alive I felt. Multi-unit ownership excited me and stretched me in ways I didn't expect. But I had no idea just how much growth—and discomfort—was waiting for me.

I'll never forget the first time I received an email from a location I had recently acquired. It was late on a Friday night, and it came from a longtime employee. She detailed how things had spiraled since my takeover. Her words stung—sharp, honest, and devastating. Reading them crushed me. My first instinct was to defend myself, to explain, to push back. But as I sat with her words, I realized something profound: being a business owner wasn't just about strategy or decisions. It required emotional resilience, humility, and the courage to face uncomfortable truths without letting them paralyze me.

There were nights when the sheer volume of responsibilities made me feel like I might implode, but every challenge was also a lesson. When acquisition opportunities came across my desk, I embraced them wholeheartedly, recognizing that growth required both risk and trust in myself. One business became three, three became five, and five eventually grew into nine, etc. Along the way, I learned that leadership is not just about running operations; it's about inspiring others, trusting your gut on someone or something, and that every obstacle is a chance to grow stronger. Balancing nursing and entrepreneurship taught me that purpose is not found in comfort, but in showing up, leaning into vulnerability, and choosing action even when fear is present.

In addition to my work as a franchise owner, I discovered a passion for business finance. I founded Free Cash Flow Advisors, a Fractional CFO firm that empowers entrepreneurs to grow with confidence—helping them understand their numbers, increase cash flow, and avoid unnecessary risks. Through my own journey and working with others, I've seen how often entrepreneurs feel lost and alone, especially when the money isn't flowing.

As of 2025, my portfolio includes eighteen brick-and-mortar locations across four brands, employing over 500 people. But beyond the numbers, what matters most to me is culture. One of our core values is Real Talk: Communicate Transparently. I want my team to feel safe to speak openly and honestly, because when people don't voice what's on their mind, small thoughts can grow into bigger problems. When we create space for honesty, we create space for growth.

If you feel like you're stuck on a hamster wheel—running endlessly on a path that isn't yours—hear this: you can step off. The wheel doesn't control you. You control whether it keeps spinning. The moment you stop running, you reclaim your power. The choice is yours.

If there's one truth I want every changemaker to carry with them, it's this: **you already hold the power to transform your life.** Not when the timing is perfect. Not when the fear disappears. Not when other people finally understand you. But now. Right now.

Because life has no rewind, no fast forward, and no pause. All you have is this moment and the choice of how to use it.

LIVE IT!

Embrace the *moment*

We are all everyday changemakers – each of us contains the ability to make an impact in our own way.

What inspired Nick to be a changemaker?

AUTHOR'S REPLY:

What inspires me to be a changemaker is my unwavering belief that people can change. I know that's not always easy to believe, but I've learned that we should never give up on others too quickly. It deeply troubles me when I see someone dismissed or avoided because of how they communicate or because of their current shortcomings. Often, these individuals are simply misunderstood. Without a strong support system, the challenges they face can grow even heavier.

That's where changemakers come in. I believe it takes empathy, patience, and genuine care to help others rise from where they are to where they can be. Time and again, I've witnessed how authentic connection and intentional action can spark real transformation—and that's incredibly rewarding. Helping others become the best version of themselves not only fulfills me, but it also creates a ripple effect that inspires more changemakers. And truly, the world needs more of them.

NOW IT IS YOUR TURN...

What inspires you to be a changemaker?

Nick invites you to reflect with two additional questions:

What is the most significant limitation that you put on yourself in the past that prevented you from experiencing an important time in your life to the fullest?

What's one of your qualities that you don't reveal to more people because you let it be overshadowed by shame?

Visit the "Meet the Changemakers" section at the back of the book to connect with and learn more about all of the authors featured in **LIVE IT!**

CHAPTER 25

Mindfulness

Creating the Everyday Changemaker

**CHANGEMAKERS: STEVEN M. COHEN,
CATHY HARTENSTEIN & CLAYTON T. PLATT**

From Steven: To everyone at Meditation4Leadership
whose passion, presence, and purpose inspire
change in others and in me.

From Cathy: To Bonnie Hartenstein, one of the
most powerful changemakers I know.

From Clayton: My wife Pamela, and adult children,
Kelsey, Taylor, and Charlie, who have supported
the changes in me.

"Lasting change, within ourselves or the world,
begins not with force, but with presence. Awareness,
curiosity, and compassion are the quiet architects
of transformation."

– STEVEN M. COHEN

Changemakers are transforming their corners of the world and beyond every day. These are ordinary people accomplishing extraordinary things—who have faced challenges, embraced resilience, and ignited global impact through their actions.

We asked corporate mindfulness facilitation leaders at Meditation4Leadership how we can each become a more impactful changemaker.

Clayton:

*D*id you ever wonder why sometimes your good intentions are never fully realized, they just sit plastered to the fridge like so many sticky notes with well-meaning platitudes? It can often boil down to a natural disconnect between a stated desire to form a new habit and the needed awareness of when, where, what, and why the behavior change should take place. That metacognition, thinking of what you are thinking, doesn't happen without practice, sometimes a lot of it. If you don't pay attention to what's happening right now, you aren't in a position to make the kinds of informed decisions that can lead to the positive results you are seeking.

Energy flows where attention goes.

I had the privilege to sit next to a very smart and interesting person at lunch a few years ago. My work had taken me to Charlotte, NC. Before the session I was leading, I was invited to join a table full of HR professionals. This person turned out to be a learning and development director, whose area of expertise was Diversity, Equity, and Inclusion. Her company was in the midst of a multi-year contract with another highly respected training company for which I had facilitated hundreds of sessions before the pandemic. We talked about how much we both respected the science behind the content, as well as the straightforward and engaging way the content was designed and delivered.

Something was missing, however, according to my lunch partner: sustained and truly measurable behavior change. Intellectually, participants of these training programs learned a lot about why and how the brain is biased and the reason we fall prey to inadvertently creating microaggressions and acting in ways that are exclusionary to specific demographic groups.

Despite being presented with solid, irrefutable evidence as well as logical "if/then" plans for how to act when situations like these arise, over the long haul, folks just reverted to their old habits. Not because they didn't care, but because they never created the habit of strengthening their "awareness muscle" so that their antennae were always ready to detect microaggressions and/or exclusionary behavior.

The question of how we put ourselves in a position to "do the right thing" and to make a positive impact, whether it's a work-related interaction or how we respond to a friend or family member amid a difficult conversation or how we help transform an organization, is often a simple matter of awareness: of the overall circumstances, of what kinds of emotions may be arising inside us that hold us back from change and recognition of the long-term positive impact exceeding the short-term pain of the change.

If we can be present enough to pay attention to all the salient inputs, we can respond in a thoughtful, circumspect manner instead of succumbing to the old flight or fight instinct. If we are aware, we can choose our focus, and armed with this power, we are much more likely to achieve our desired results, in this case, being an impactful change maker.

Cathy:

Sometimes, I think the best way to be a changemaker is to do absolutely nothing.

"Hold on," you're thinking, "how can that be?" But hear me out.

Not too long ago, the company I had worked at for ten years was sold, leading to a period of intense transition. Every day was filled with unpredictability, change, and confusion. This triggered my deep need to hold on—to control, to find normalcy in a sea of uncertainty.

What I noticed was that when I fixated on a struggle or obstacle, it became my focus. The more I concentrated on the gap—the distance between where I was and where I wanted to be—instead of embracing the present moment, the more my goals slipped farther away. Eventually, I found myself going in circles, winding up exactly where I had started.

For much of my life, I felt caught between the past and the future, struggling to stay present. I believe the speed at which we live is one of the biggest obstacles to being fully engaged in the moment. We rush from task to task, preoccupied with our to-do lists, responsibilities, and distractions. So much energy is spent on achieving, succeeding, and producing—always doing, doing, doing. But ultimately, we need to stop, listen, breathe, and do nothing. In other words, we must surrender to the present moment.

Yet, this proves to be one of the greatest challenges for most of us. How do we navigate our hectic lives while remaining grounded in the now? How do we let go of past fears and hurts that weigh us down? How do we release the daily anxieties and stresses, trusting that the universe will take care of us?

This is where a strong meditation and mindfulness practice becomes invaluable. I've found that if I take just a few moments to breathe, slow down, and fully notice what is happening in the present, I can reconnect with myself and regain clarity. Meditation and mindfulness provide an opportunity to release stress, find stillness, and return to what truly matters.

When you slow down and fully engage with each moment, something miraculous happens: your mind clears, and your actions become more effective. Patience reveals itself, reminding you of what is important and what is not. You realize that control is an illusion—that constantly trying to manage everything leads to anxiety and stress and distances you from truly experiencing life. Challenges will always be there, some days more intensely than others. But when we pause, breathe, and connect with ourselves, we create space for new possibilities and opportunities we might have otherwise missed.

So, the next time you feel overwhelmed, stressed, or out of sorts, slow down. Take a moment. Look around. Breathe. In any given moment, there are countless opportunities for gratitude, love, connection, and joy. Yet, we often overlook them, rushing on to the next thing. We fear that if we fully embrace the present, everything demanding our attention will suffer. But the truth is, we suffer most when we ignore the present and postpone our happiness for the future. When we commit to experiencing the here and now, we open ourselves to possibilities we never knew existed.

Change often tempts us to resist or retreat, but what if, instead, we leaned into it? By moving toward change rather than away from it, we open doors we never imagined possible. When faced with challenges, we must take a moment to surrender, listen to our inner wisdom, and respond in a way that allows us to seize the opportunities before us. In doing so, we embrace our role as changemakers—both in our own lives and within our communities.

Steve:

One of my favorite Broadway show titles is the 1980s musical *I Love You, You're Perfect, Now Change,* about NYC couples growing over time from dating to old age. My wife and I will often use this phrase when trying to cajole each other to do something differently. The key "aha" moment for me was to recognize that a willingness to change doesn't mean that there is something wrong with me, and a willingness to change or evolve best practices in an organization doesn't mean the people that are currently engaging in the existing practices are not performing well.

Life gives us plenty of opportunities every day to create the change we want to see. I find the trick is to be sufficiently aware to see these opportunities to be able to act on them. Whether the change is small or big; whether the change is for yourself, adding value for someone with whom you are in relationship or your community; or whether you are changing something you notice for the first time or a long-standing issue, the hardest part is often being aware of what needs to be done and what you can do in that moment to help you get there.

Meditation is the practice that has helped me strengthen my mind muscle to build that awareness. A little bit of strength training to practice observing in the present moment with full attention and without judgment. Meditation practice works for your mind just like a gym workout strengthens the body. A daily practice. Sometimes you may fall out of practice and then start to notice you just aren't moving through life the same way. Start again. Build back the mindfulness muscle. Notice the greater awareness, connection, balance, and ability to see things as they really are.

I will tell you a secret (I guess it isn't really a secret if I am publishing it in this article). When a meditation facilitator instructs us to "focus on our breath," my mind often wanders after a few moments. Over time, I learned two tricks. The first is not to be judgmental about my failure to be able to focus on my breath for longer periods of time – a practice of self-compassion. The second is to recognize when my mind strays and simply come back to focus on my breath, no matter how many times that happens. Third, to add "something else" to my breath focus, such as counting or a mantra.

Mantra meditation is a focus on a word, phrase, or saying that returns one to a state of focus, balance, and equanimity. Sometimes a mantra is simply a series of sounds or vibrations. Sometimes a mantra itself has deep meaning. My favorite mantras serve three primary purposes: (i) rhythmic, (ii) reinforce meaning, and (iii) a focal point that I can align with my breath.

Over time, one of my favorite mantras has become what I refer to as the "Changemaker Mantra." It was originally inspired by the famous quote often attributed to Mahatma Gandhi: "Be the change that you wish to see in the world." Gandhi emphasized the importance of personal transformation as a catalyst for global change.

I start my practice by sitting upright with good posture, grounded on the floor or a chair. I begin to notice my breath, without changing it, and am often amazed that I was previously breathing the same way without noticing (what else don't I notice?). Noticing the inhale, the brief pause between the inhale and the exhale, the exhale, and the brief pause between the exhale and the next inhale (noting the metaphorical importance of the pause). As I proceed, I add the following mantra rhythmically with my breath:

(inhale) **Be the Change**
(Pause)
(Exhale) **I Wish to See**
(Pause)
(Inhale) **Both in the World**
(Pause)
(Exhale) **And Within Me**
(Pause)
Repeat as often as desired.

It actually took me a year (and suggestions from my Practical Mantra program participants) to get the words just right so they have perfect rhythm and meaning to help me maintain my focus and to reinforce the mantra message.

Over time, I have learned that I am not perfect (still far from it). That doesn't make me a bad or weak person or performer. I have become more aware when change is needed and when and why I am resistant to certain changes (sometimes the resistance still wins out). Effective leaders adapt proactively. Change requires taking risks. Sometimes those risks fail. That doesn't make the risk taker a failure. Change leads to struggle; struggle makes us stronger. Changemakers recognize and overcome the struggle. Changemakers have a growth mindset that leads to positive impact. Creating more mindful changemakers is the change we wish to see in the world.

About Meditation4Leadership:

Meditation4Leadership exists to support people in becoming the best version of themselves – at work, at home, and in life. We offer a space to pause, reflect, and reconnect with what truly matters, using meditation and mindfulness as practical tools to build awareness, deepen connection, and foster emotional well-being. Our work is rooted in the understanding that leadership is not just about titles or outcomes, it's about presence, perspective, and the ability to respond with clarity and compassion in every moment.

Through our programs, we guide individuals and teams in developing skills that are often overlooked in traditional leadership development: the ability to listen with empathy, to manage stress effectively, to lead with purpose, and to create environments where people feel seen, heard, and valued. In a world that moves fast and demands more, Meditation4Leadership offers a path back to balance—a way to lead from within, with intention, integrity, and heart.

LIVE IT!
Embrace the *moment*

We are all everyday changemakers – each of us contains the ability to make an impact in our own way.

What inspired Steven, Cathy, & Clayton to be a changemakers?

STEVEN'S REPLY:
We each have the potential to make a positive impact every day. We also have the potential to assist, uplift and support others to effectuate their positive impact. I am inspired every day by the potential of others and try to do what I can to add value to effectuate positive change in the world.

CATHY'S REPLY:
The deep belief that every individual carries a unique spark of brilliance—and that true transformation begins from within. With over 25 years of experience in education, coaching, and leadership development, I've seen how empowering people to gain clarity, confidence, and self-awareness creates ripple effects that extend far beyond the individual. My work with Meditation4Leadership fuels this passion. Lasting change isn't about quick fixes—it's about deep, sustainable growth. When individuals are truly empowered, they become changemakers in their own right—and that kind of collective transformation has the power to shift entire systems.

CLAYTON'S REPLY:

I believe awareness is the most underappreciated catalyst for meaningful change. Whether it's helping someone notice the subtle ways they might unintentionally exclude others, or guiding them to tune into their own thoughts and emotions before they act, I've seen again and again how paying attention changes everything.

NOW IT IS YOUR TURN...

What inspires you to be a changemaker?

Steve, Cathy & Clayton invite you to reflect on these additional questions:

In what areas of your life could building your "awareness muscle" help close the gap between your good intentions and your everyday actions?

How might being more present to your thoughts, emotions, and surroundings empower you to create more inclusive, compassionate, and authentic connections?

Visit the "Meet the Changemakers" section at the back of the book to connect with and learn more about all of the authors featured in **LIVE IT!**

CHAPTER 26

From Shadows to Spotlight: *Empowering* Uganda's Forgotten Girls and Women

CHANGEMAKER: CHRISTINE NAMUSAAZI

To my daughter, Namutebi Maria Praise. I believe she
will one day be a changemaker. Also to my mum,
Mrs. Florence Nakabuye Ssenkami

"Empowering a woman is not just lifting her;
it is planting seeds of change that grow into
stronger communities, brighter futures, and a
world where every girl can rise."

– CHRISTINE NAMUSAAZI

*I*n the heart of Uganda, where rolling hills and rural landscapes meet bustling towns and under-resourced communities, a quiet revolution is taking shape. It is not waged with weapons or fanfare, but with scissors, braids, notebooks, and a profound sense of purpose. It is a revolution led by She Unit Uganda, an organization built on an unwavering belief that every girl and woman, regardless of their educational background or social status, deserves dignity, opportunity, and hope.

Many of the girls and women we serve were once invisible to the system meant to support them—some were forced to drop out of school due to poverty, early marriage, domestic violence, or teenage pregnancy. Others were never given the chance to begin. For them, life felt like a closed door, a series of missed opportunities and silent dreams. But at She Unit Uganda, we see them clearly, we see their strength, their potential, and their right to thrive. We work every day to ensure that the rest of the world sees them too.

As the founder of She Unit Uganda, I know what it means to rise from difficulty. My life's journey gave me a deep understanding of barriers faced by girls and women in Uganda.

After graduating from a cosmetology program, I began training young women and girls free of charge. I did this because I deeply understood the pain of wanting to achieve something in life but being unable to afford it. I remember those years when I desperately searched for a university scholarship.

That struggle gave me the strength to start She Unit Uganda in 2018. I knew there were women and girls out there facing even harder situations than mine, and I wanted to create a space where they could find hope and skills to survive and thrive.

In 2019, just when I had given up on the dream of going to university, I met someone who changed my life. Through his organization, I received funds, part of which was to support She Unit Uganda, and the rest was to pay my tuition. I finally started studying in 2020. But shortly after, COVID-19 hit, and everything came to a halt.

I had entrusted my tuition savings to someone for safekeeping, but life took a painful turn. In October 2020, I fell ill with a mysterious illness for which none of the treatments worked. My family couldn't keep up with the costs of continuous treatment. Slowly, I began using my tuition and every cent I received on medication and care. By the end of 2020, I had spent nearly $3,000, and I still wasn't healed.

Being from Africa, my mother was advised to take me to a spiritualist. At that time, I was unconscious and unaware of what was happening. I only remember regaining consciousness one Friday on our way to the spiritualist's home. I was hallucinating, pale, and freezing cold. When we arrived, out of fear, my mother agreed to everything. We paid a hefty sum, hoping I would be healed. I was terrified, but I wanted to live. My mother's fear was even greater. I could see it in her eyes.

That's how I lost the money meant for my education and the trust of someone who had believed in me. I couldn't explain to him that the money was spent on treatment and desperate attempts to save my life. I hated myself. I was disappointed in God. For a young woman who had just begun to touch her dreams, it felt like I had lost everything, and I still wasn't completely healed.

In December 2020, a psychiatrist diagnosed me with chronic anxiety disorder. It was a turning point. But this new reality meant even more medical costs, therapy, medication, and endless visits. I had no savings left, but fortunately, in early 2021, we secured a partnership that allowed me to earn an income. Still, it wasn't enough.

Living with chronic anxiety was brutal. I experienced severe panic attacks, dizziness, blurred vision, brain fog, and derealization. My body was always overheating. My head burned constantly. But I had to keep working, because if I didn't, I couldn't pay for treatment. That entire year, I was just trying to survive.

Even at school, I struggled. I couldn't focus. I didn't make any friends. I just sat there, staring at the teacher while my mind drifted endlessly. That same year, She Unit Uganda had the highest number of beneficiaries; yet I don't remember most of their faces. That's how deeply I was affected.

Eventually, we lost the partnership. I tried to explain, but part of me was relieved; I needed rest. In just two years, I had lost my scholarship, my savings, my health, and my peace. I had missed several papers at university and had to take a semester off.

It was overwhelming, but I refused to give up.

She Unit's vision was simple: to offer second chances, to provide practical skills, mentorship, and sisterhood of support for girls and women who had been excluded and underestimated. From its earliest days, the organization focused on reaching out to those in the shadows, the school dropouts, the young mothers, the survivors of gender-based violence, and the marginalized rural youth.

It wasn't easy, but with an abundance of determination, She Unit Uganda began offering free vocational training in cosmetology. Additionally, it offered skills in how to make hair shampoo, conditioner, and liquid soap. What started as a small initiative grew into a vibrant movement of women uplifting women.

Some of the most transformative programs we have launched to date were made possible by grants from A Chance in Life in 2021, Today is the Day Changemakers Grant, and continuous support from Women and Girls Education International. With their generous support, we have been able to train over 400 young women and girls in cosmetology, a skill that not only brings beauty but also income, dignity, and independence.

Before the training, many of the girls had never held a hairdryer, let alone styled a client. Some had been sitting at home, unemployed and uncertain about the future; others had been working odd jobs for meager pay, barely enough to survive. But once they entered our training space, everything began to change.

We trained them in hairdressing, braiding, scalp treatment, makeup application, nail care, and hygiene. More importantly, we empowered them with business skills, how to manage clients, calculate profits, and market their services.

We have watched with joy as women who once saw themselves as failures blossom into confident beauticians. Some of them started home-based salons; others joined existing businesses; a few came together to form their own cooperatives. Their transformation was not only economic; it was emotional and spiritual. They were no longer invisible; they were skilled professionals, standing proudly in the spotlight.

Although we have made progress, the challenges in our country continue to burden many women. Education is their only way out.

Condition of Uneducated Girls in Uganda

Uganda, like many sub-Saharan African countries, faces significant challenges related to girls' education. Many girls are either pushed out of school early or never have the opportunity to attend at all. This lack of education often exposes them to a cycle of poverty, early marriage, exploitation, and gender-based violence.

Key Statistics

1. **Out-of-school girls**:
    Recent estimates by UNESCO and Uganda Bureau of Statistics (UBOS) indicate over 1.2 million girls aged six to eighteen years are out of school in Uganda.
    Girls are more likely to drop out than boys, especially during adolescence.

2. **Early marriages and teenage pregnancy:**
    One in four girls is married before eighteen.
    Teenage pregnancy remains high, with 25% of Ugandan girls aged fifteen to nineteen already mothers or pregnant.
    These factors are leading causes of school dropout among girls.

3. **Dropout by education level:**
    By secondary school, less than 30% of Ugandan girls remain enrolled.
    Many girls leave school between five and primary seven due to school fees, menstruation challenges, and domestic responsibilities.

4. **Menstruation and period poverty:**
    Over 60% of girls in rural areas miss school during menstruation due to a lack of sanitary pads or clean facilities.
    Some girls miss up to five days of school per month, contributing to poor performance and dropouts.

5. **Literacy rates:**
    Female literacy in Uganda (ages fifteen to twenty-four) stands at about 84%, but in rural or impoverished regions, it drops significantly.

6. **Impact of COVID-19:**
   Prolonged school closures (2020-2022) resulted in many girls not returning to school.
   An estimated 30% of girls who dropped out of school during COVID-19 have not returned due to early pregnancies, child marriage, or economic hardships.

What Needs to Be Done

1. Access to vocational training for out-of-school girls (like what She Unit Uganda provides)
2. Free or subsidized education, especially in secondary school
3. Menstrual hygiene support and access to reproductive health education
4. Community sensitization on the value of educating girls
5. Safe spaces for girls to learn and grow, especially for survivors of violence or teen mothers.

Consequences of Being Uneducated for Girls in Uganda

Lack of education among girls in Uganda has far-reaching effects, not only on the girls themselves but also on their families, communities, and the nation at large.

Some of the most critical consequences include the following:

1. Early Marriage and Teenage Pregnancy

Uneducated girls are more likely to be married off early or become pregnant as teenagers. Without education, they lack the knowledge and power to make informed decisions about their lives.

2. Poverty and Unemployment

Without skills or qualifications, uneducated girls struggle to find decent jobs. Most end up in informal, low-paying work or complete dependency, remaining trapped in poverty.

3. Poor Health and Hygiene

Uneducated girls are less informed about reproductive health, menstrual hygiene, and nutrition. This puts them at higher risk of diseases, early motherhood, complications, and poor mental health.

4. Gender-Based Violence and Exploitation

Girls who are uneducated are more vulnerable to sexual exploitation, trafficking, and domestic abuse. They often lack knowledge about their rights or how to seek help. Many remain trapped in abusive relationships due to financial dependence.

5. Social Exclusion and Low Self-Esteem

Many uneducated girls face stigma and are seen as failures or burdens. They suffer from low self-worth, depression, and hopelessness. They often live in isolation, lacking peer networks or mentors.

. Cycle of Disempowerment

When a girl is uneducated, the next generation is also at risk. Children of uneducated mothers are more likely to be malnourished, unvaccinated, and uneducated. The impact is multigenerational, reinforcing inequality.

7. National Impact

When girls are excluded from education, Uganda loses human capital. It slows economic growth, increases dependency rates, and weakens national development. According to the World Bank, each additional year of schooling for a girl can increase her future earnings by 10-20%.

Our Vision for the Future

At She Unit Ugnada, we envision a future where no girl or woman is left behind, where those who missed out on formal education are not forgotten but empowered to rise. We aim to expand our vocational training programs to reach more underserved communities across Uganda, with a focus on practical, marketable skills like cosmetology, liquid soap and shampoo making, financial literacy, and eventually, reusable pads production. We are also looking at tailoring as a skill to teach.

Our dream is to establish a fully equipped Women's Empowerment and Training Center that serves as a safe, inclusive space for learning, healing, and economic transformation.

Beyond skills, our vision includes a deeper advocacy, mentorship, and community engagement. We want to influence policy, challenge harmful gender norms, and raise awareness about the value of investing in girls and women.

Through strategic partnership and grassroots mobilization, we plan to scale our impact, ensuring every woman we touch becomes a change agent in her family and community. With the right support, we believe Uganda can be a place where girls move from margins to the mainstream, not only surviving but leading.

As for me, I resumed school in 2022 and completed all the papers I had missed. I graduated in 2025. My hope is still alive. Despite everything I've been through, I still believe I will rise again.

LIVE IT!

Embrace the *moment*

We are all everyday changemakers – each of us contains the ability to make an impact in our own way.

What inspired Christine to be a changemaker?

AUTHOR'S REPLY:

I was born in a family of nine children, but only three of us made it to high school. Growing up, we often went to school hungry because my mother couldn't afford breakfast or lunch, and as a result, I developed ulcers at a young age, but I pushed through. Through sponsorship, I completed school. During holidays I helped my sponsor on farms and catering events to pay my school fees. Later, I took up hairdressing so I could support my siblings' education and myself. While I don't regret helping them, it meant putting my own dreams on hold. But those struggles shaped my purpose. No child should go to school hungry. No girl should miss education because of poverty. And no mother should lack the skills to support her family. That's why I started She Unit Uganda—to give marginalized women free vocational training. Because when you empower a mother, you empower an entire family. And when families are lifted, children get the chance to dream without limits. Today, I share my skills freely so others can build a better life.

NOW IT IS YOUR TURN...

What inspires you to be a changemaker?

Christine invites you to reflect with two additional questions:

How can empowering women and girls in one community influence global efforts toward gender equality, economic growth, and climate action?

What roles should individuals, governments, and international organizations play in ensuring marginalized women and girls worldwide have access to education, skills, and resources?

Visit the "Meet the Changemakers" section at the back of the book to connect with and learn more about all of the authors featured in **LIVE IT!**

CHAPTER 27

Your Invitation to Live It!

Your Way

CHANGEMAKER: JODI HOPE GRINWALD

To my dad, who I miss every single day: you taught me to practice the religion of kindness, and that life is about conversation, a hug, and showing up. I carry all of the lessons you taught me and share them with others as often as I can.

"Surround yourself with those who truly see you—
those who honor your heart, challenge your growth,
and walk beside you with kindness. "

– JODI HOPE GRINWALD

ou've spent time reading stories of courage, creativity, leadership, and everyday impact.

This final chapter is about you, whether you're ready for your next step, needing a moment to pause, or standing in that space of uncertainty where you feel called toward something but aren't yet sure how to reach it.

Thirty-One Voices Beside You

Thirty-one changemaker voices opened their hearts in these pages. They shared their lessons, their vulnerability, their strength, and their losses, not to be placed on a pedestal, but to sit beside you. Every voice in this book came together for one purpose: to offer something that might help you feel connected, reminded, encouraged, or seen. None of them claimed perfection. None of them waited to feel ready. They simply chose to share what life taught them, hoping their words would find you in the moment you needed them most.

Your story matters. It doesn't have to look like anyone else's. It just has to be yours: honest, real, and not weighed down by someone else's expectations or judgments. I was taught not to give advice, but to offer observations. Advice can come with pressure or judgment if it isn't followed. Observations are different. You get to take what fits, leave what doesn't, and make your own meaning from it.

So here is one of my observations: do not let the weight of another person's opinion dim your light. Remember that how someone sees you, your choices, or your path is a reflection of their lens, not your worth. Their perspective belongs to them. You are the one who has to live your life. The lens that matters most, the one you must keep coming back to, is your own.

Starting from Nothing and Moving Through Fear

So much of real connection, real life-shifting connection, begins with the courage to start something from nothing. To take the first step when the outcome is unclear. To ask for support even when your voice shakes. To believe that you are allowed to want what you want, to ask for what you deserve, and to take that leap of faith toward the thing that keeps calling to you.

Everything I've built, the podcast, the forum, the coaching and consulting work, this whole ecosystem, started from that place. A blank page. A quiet idea. A feeling that something more was possible mixed with the fear of not knowing how to begin, how to build what I imagined, and how others might judge the choices I was making. Connection grew in the moments when I finally spoke up, asked for help, or reached out to someone I admired. Momentum came from the times I said yes even when I was scared, or no when it would have been easier to stay small.

What I hope you take from this book is that being a changemaker or a heart-centered leader doesn't always require big gestures. Sometimes the most powerful shift begins with one small decision: sending the email, opening the door, offering a smile, taking the class, saying yes, saying no, or simply allowing yourself to believe that what you feel called toward is valid in your life, your work, and your leadership.

I wish I could say I always knew how to take those steps, but I didn't. For a long time I waited, waited for courage, waited for clarity, waited for the right moment. It took a life-changing event for me to finally move toward something I knew deep down I was meant to do. I don't want that for you. You don't need a crisis to choose yourself. You just need one moment where you decide that your voice deserves space.

If I had ignored that moment, this ecosystem that now supports so many people might never have formed. Connection is not just philosophy. It is a lifeline. It's the thing that carries us when titles won't, when metrics do not measure what matters, and when the table gets quiet and we are left facing our own truth.

Tables, Fit, and the Messy Middle

And just a quick reminder: some tables are simply not a fit for you, and that is okay. If you aren't given the space to be heard or your contributions don't feel valued, it may be time to give your seat to someone else. That isn't a reflection of your worth; it's a reflection of the table. It may be a sign that it's time to move toward a table that feels aligned, or, as we talked about in Chapter Two, that you may be called to build a table or two of your own. When you finally find or create a table where you belong, you don't have to shrink. You breathe easier. You rise. You contribute. You create connection that changes outcomes for you and for others.

Maybe you're in the messy middle right now, that foggy place between what was and what could be. It can feel uncomfortable and uncertain, but the messy middle isn't a detour. It's where the groundwork is laid. Everything you're carrying, your questions, courage, values, and hopes, is not a burden; it's building material.

Let go of what no longer serves you, keep what does, and take one small step. It sounds simple, but the truth is that it isn't. How do you let go without fearing judgment? You do it by remembering this: if you don't let go of what no longer serves you, the whispers will eventually become screams. The disappointment, overwhelm, and sadness you feel at times will continue. It is only when you honor yourself and give yourself permission to release what is weighing you down that you create room to move forward. When you choose yourself, even quietly, even imperfectly, you begin to open the space needed for that next step to reveal itself.

Staying Connected to What Grounds You

And if you can't find that feeling right now, if the days are heavy and you don't know how to reach for that moment, go back to the places that remind you of who you are. Read this book again. Listen to a motivational speaker. Reach out to a mentor. Call a friend who will truly listen.

For me I feel most connected after a podcast interview, a session with a coaching client, immediately after the Changemakers Forum each year, or when I see a child connect with music. When I feel overwhelmed by all that I hold, coaching, consulting, podcast hosting, serving as CEO of a nonprofit, creating an ecosystem, as soon as I have one truly connective conversation, it becomes fuel for me to keep moving forward. It brings me to a feeling of deep fulfillment, and I am so grateful for that. On a personal note, spending time with my family, my friends, and now my beautiful grandbaby, those moments are gifts I hold close.

Life also moves in seasons, much like the weather. Some days feel bright and steady; others arrive heavy, overcast, or unclear. The feelings don't stay fixed, even when it seems like they will. When you notice the moments that bring you into your flow, the conversations, the work, the creativity, or the quiet pauses where you feel most present, pay attention. Those moments are guideposts. They can help you remember who you are and gently point you toward your next step, especially on the days when everything feels cloudy or slow to shift.

As this book comes to a close, I want you to return to the people you've met in these pages. Leaders, dreamers, creatives, survivors, visionaries, each of them took a step that changed something in their life or in the life of someone else. Their stories are reminders that impact doesn't require a stage. It often happens at a kitchen table, in a hallway conversation, in a moment of honesty, or in a quiet decision no one else sees. That's where real change begins.

Learn more about the voices in this book by turning to the Meet the Changemakers section, where you'll see the impact they are making every day. And if you have a story of your own, a message, a moment, a shift, I would love to share it through the Today is the Day ecosystem and invite you to become part of it. The podcast, the forum, The Connective, and all of the spaces we are building are designed for heart-centered humans from all levels and walks of life who truly want to learn and grow together. Your voice is welcome here.

Your Voice as the Thirty-Second Voice

Possibility didn't come naturally to me. I wasn't someone who grew up believing I could do anything. But somewhere along the journey, piece by piece, through connection, courage, and choosing what felt true, I learned that so much more is possible than I ever imagined.

And I believe that for you, too.

Before you close this book, pause with me one more time: If you were the thirty-second voice in this book, adding your chapter to the story of stepping beyond the edge of comfort and into the center of impact in your life, your work, and the world around you, what would you want it to say?

We are all ready to meet you,
every voice you've met in these pages,
at the edge of your comfort zone,
where your courage begins,
and in the center of impact,
where your leadership takes root.

We have a seat at our table waiting just for you.

Today is the day!

LIVE IT!

Embrace the *moment*

We are all everyday changemakers – each of us contains the ability to make an impact in our own way.

What inspires you to be a changemaker?

Jodi invites you to reflect with two additional questions:

Which authors did you connect with most, and how did their lessons or experiences inspire you to think differently about something in your own life or work?

What are you doing right now to move closer to the impact, connection, or change you want to create, and what will help you stay true to that when challenges show up?

Visit the "Meet the Changemakers" section at the back of the book to connect with and learn more about all of the authors featured in **LIVE IT!**

Acknowledgments

There are so many hearts and hands behind this book that I need to acknowledge.

First and foremost, to the thirty-one changemaker voices who turned this from an idea into the book you are reading today. I am endlessly grateful to know you and to have you in my life. Thank you for your courage, sharing your vulnerability, your honesty, and your heart.

To Heather McCulloch, what a journey this has been. Thank you for saying yes, for staying in it with me, and for working so hard to bring this project to life. I am profoundly grateful for your partnership and belief in this vision.

To Design 446, Ann Marie, Allison, and the entire team, I am truly grateful and blessed to have had you on this project, and hopefully on many more to come. From the book cover to the decorative pages, the line art, and the thoughtful advice along the way, your creative fingerprints are everywhere. It is priceless to have a team that supports you with such care and patience. You see my vision before I do, and that is a rare gift.

To Marie at Books to Hook Publishing, thank you for your patience, your time, and your expertise. You helped shape this book into something truly special, and your steady guidance behind the scenes made all the difference.

To my husband, Dave, for saying, "You already have a book with all these changemakers in your sphere." Those words were a spark that helped me see what was possible and move this from concept to creation. Thank you for your love, our vacations, your precious gifts, and your incredible hugs. Love you!

To my stepdaughter, Charlotte, thank you for the fun times we had keeping track of the authors who signed on to be part of this project. I adore spending time with you.

To my mom, my rock, our family matriarch, and the strong woman who is always there when you need her to listen and hold space. Your example of resilience and unconditional love is at the core of who I am.

To my sister Melissa, my brother-in-law Ray, and my niece Isabella, thank you for always giving me and my kiddos a soft place to land, no matter what. Knowing we can always count on your support is a gift we never take for granted.

To Jimmie & Tony Marra, your support means the world to me and I am so grateful to have you in my life.

To my incredible friends, Sandee and Neela, thank you for cheering me on, no matter what I do, where I go, or how I get there, and doing so without judgment. That is a true gift! Your friendship is a constant source of strength.

To the many mentors who have walked beside me over the years, I could never list you all by name, but please know that each of you has helped bring me to this moment. I have already woven many of you on these pages.

Fred Wasiak, who so generously wrote the foreword for this book, carries the same principles of kindness and presence that shaped so much of my own life. I am so beyond grateful for all the time and belief he has given to me through the years.

My hope is that everyone reading this book finds someone, whether through friendship, leadership, or coaching, who helps them connect to their inner truth and ignite their own momentum. People who help you uncover what already lives within you, who challenge you to grow, and who show you that what you learn from others can become the spark that turns you into a changemaker in your own corner of the world.

Meet the Author & Curator

Jodi Hope Grinwald, CPC, ELI-MP
Leadership & Connection Strategist |
Certified Professional Coach |
Author | Podcast Host
Energy Leadership Index Master
Practitioner | Changemaker |
Nonprofit Leader

Jodi is the founder of Today is the Day, an ecosystem dedicated to elevating voices, strengthening leadership, and advancing meaningful human connection. She is the visionary behind *Today is the Day: Live It!,* the author of its signature chapters, the creator of the International Changemakers Forum, and host of the Today is the Day Changemakers Podcast, reaching listeners in more than 135 countries. She is also launching the Today is the Day Changemakers Connective, a community designed to inspire growth, collaboration, and impact.

Through her connection-centered approach, Jodi helps leaders lead more effectively, supports entrepreneurs in growing their businesses, and equips teams to strengthen communication, alignment, and performance all while ensuring bottom-line sustainability and growth.

Jodi is the co-founder and CEO of the Zzak G. Applaud Our Kids Foundation, which funds ongoing performing arts education for children ages 7–18 who meet financial-need criteria in New Jersey.

A Professional Member of the Recording Academy, Jodi has been recognized with the 2024 Jersey Shore's Most Influential in Business Award, the 2023 New Jersey Governor's Award in Arts Education, and the 2021 Athena Leadership Award.

Across every platform, she champions one essential truth: **connection drives everything in our lives — how we lead, how we communicate, and how we create meaningful impact.**

Facebook: Today is the Day Live It
Facebook: Zzak G. Applaud Our Kids Foundation
Instagram: todayisthedayliveit
Instagram: applaudourkids
LinkedIn: Jodi Grinwald
LinkedIn: Zzak G. Applaud Our Kids
YouTube: Today is the Day Changemakers
todayisthedayliveit.com
applaudourkids.org

Meet the Editor

Heather McCulloch

Writer/Former Reuters Journalist; President, Women & Girls Education International; Board Member, Native American Intertribal Caucus; Certified Health Coach

Heather is a professional writer, certified tutor, editor, and proud mother of a son who is pursuing a career in forensic mental health counseling. Striving to be a champion for human rights and an advocate for those less fortunate, she co-founded and serves as president for the nonprofit, Women & Girls Education International, which is committed to ending or preventing violence against women and girls through education. She also serves on the board of the Native American Intertribal Caucus, where her emphasis is on communications and addressing the missing and murdered Indigenous women and girls. In March 2026, she will also be a certified Integrated Nutrition Health Coach. With more than 30 years in the writing field, she has managed a monthly newspaper, launched a newsletter; managed a team of journalists, written for a worldwide news service, Reuters, and managed an alumni magazine. She has also volunteered for social services, tutored math and

English to junior high school students in Washington, DC, taught English as a second language to a Taiwanese minister, and, since 2020, has delivered for Meals on Wheels.

Facebook: Pressing Releases
Instagram: pressingreleases and wageintl
LinkedIn: Heather Mistretta
wageinternational.org
pressingreleases.com

Meet The Changemaker
Voices of Live It!

Amy Wachtel Delman
Owner, Amy Delman Public Relations

Amy is a public relations consultant with more than three decades of experience in PR, marketing, and branding. She specializes in using media exposure to raise awareness and drive revenue, with her work featured in publications including *The New York Times*, *The Star-Ledger*, NJBIZ, ROI-NJ, Inc., and the *National Journal of Public Relations*. A lifelong poet, Amy has been published in outlets such as *AUTHORITY* magazine, *The National Library of Poetry*, and various anthologies. In 2021, she penned the foreword—in verse—for a consumer lifestyle book that sold over 1,000 copies in its first quarter. For more than thirty years, she has owned a custom poetry business and now shares her work through a poetry blog on Instagram under a pen name.

LinkedIn: Amy Delman
Instagram: amydelmanpr
Facebook: Amy Delman Public Relations LLC
X: amydelmanpr
amydelmanpr.com

Ann Marie Baker
Vice President, Design 446

For nearly forty years, Ann Marie has consulted and managed marketing projects for some of the largest names in the homebuilding industry, including K. Hovnanian Companies, Lennar, and Pulte Homes. Through her leadership, Design 446 has garnered numerous local, state, and national awards. In addition to working with the company's core business clientele, Ann Marie has expanded the client base to include a myriad of new business start-ups and company rebrands.

As a volunteer, Ann Marie proudly sits on multiple nonprofit boards/committees, including HOPE Sheds Light, Ocean County YMCA, JBJ Soul Foundation Advisory Board, Ocean's Harbor House Advisory Board, and the Greater Toms River Chamber of Commerce nonprofit committee.

LinkedIn: Design 446
Facebook: Design 446
Instagram: design446
design446.com

Catherine Curry-Williams
Cofounder, She Angels Foundation;
Founder, Shane's Inspiration; TEDx
Speaker & Bestselling Author

Catherine "Cat" is a TEDx speaker, bestselling author, and keynote presenter. A force for positive change, she inspires others by believing that meaningful change is possible at any scale, fostering connections that spark shared purpose and action. In 1997, she founded Shane's Inspiration in memory of her son, leading a global movement to build inclusive sensory- and literacy-rich playgrounds where children of all abilities can play together. In 2020, she co-founded the She Angels Foundation, providing monthly grants to grassroots organizations that support women and girls. Honored as a L'Oréal Paris "Woman of Worth," California "Woman of the Year," and recipient of the Lifetime Achievement Award from President Barack Obama, Cat's bestselling book, *Philanthropy on a Shoestring*, shows that every act of giving matters.

LinkedIn: Catherine Curry-Williams
Instagram: @catcurrywilliams
Facebook: Cat Curry-Williams
catherinecurrywilliams.com

Cathy Hartenstein
Life and Leadership Coach, Create More Bliss. Cohost, Women Arising Podcast; Facilitator, Meditation for Leadership

Cathy is a dedicated facilitator, educator, and coach with more than thirty years of experience in leadership development, education, and meditation. As a facilitator for Meditation4Leadership, she helps leaders deepen awareness, presence, and emotional intelligence through mindfulness-based practices that inspire conscious, compassionate leadership. Formerly the director of professional development at E-Therapy, Cathy led initiatives that strengthened leadership, communication, and well-being for educators nationwide. A certified practitioner in EFT, Matrix Reimprinting, and NLP, she guides individuals to unlock their potential through transformational life coaching. She co-hosts the *Woman Arising* podcast, inspiring women to live with purpose and possibility. Cathy has taught at leading universities, including the University of Arizona and the University of Colorado, and holds an MFA in Directing. Based in Sedona, AZ, she weaves vision, creativity, and presence into her work, helping people create meaningful, lasting change from the inside out.

Facebook: Meditation4Leadership
Instagram: meditation4leadership
LinkedIn: Meditation4Leadership
YouTube: @meditation4leadership
X: Meditation4lead
Meditation4Leadership.org

Charlene Gorzela
Midlife/Third Act Coach,
Leadership Consultant, Speaker
- Life Reinvention Now

Charlene specializes in inside/out living by activating the pure potentiality of men and women who want to live extraordinary lives—personally and professionally—especially in their Midlife or Third Act. A coach, consultant, and speaker, she blends business acumen with Positive Intelligence™ and cutting-edge biohacking strategies. Through her practice, she helps individuals and small business leaders activate life from the inside out—rewiring mental habits, quieting inner saboteurs, and optimizing the body at the cellular level for lasting energy, resilience, and clarity, and with some fun/laughter thrown in!

As a consultant with a leader in health activation, Charlene furthers her mission to help others live with greater healthspan—not just lifespan.

Facebook: Charlene Gorzela
Instagram: charlene_gorzela
LinkedIn: Charlene Gorzela
LifeReinventionNow.com

Chaya Pamula
Cofounder, President & CEO, PamTen Inc.; Founder, SOFKIN & SheTek

Chaya is a visionary technologist, serial entrepreneur, and humanitarian who seamlessly fuses innovation with purpose. As Co-Founder, President, and CEO of PamTen Inc (www.pamten.com) and SMAC Apps (www.smacapps.ai) , she shapes and delivers end-to-end technology solutions including digital, AI, and professional staffing services across the U.S., Canada, and India.

Chaya serves on several corporate and nonprofit boards advancing technology, education, and inclusive community development. She holds an MBA, Bank Director Certification, and has completed executive program at Harvard Business School and the Goldman Sachs 10,000 Small Businesses program, bringing together strategic rigor and entrepreneurial foresight.

Being a philanthropist and passionate changemaker, she founded two not-for profit organizations - SOFKIN (www.sofkin.org) to provide loving homes and holistic care for underserved children in India, and SHETEK (www.shetek.net) to empower and elevate women in technology. A sought-after speaker at the United Nations, Harvard India Conference, and global forums, Chaya has been honored as a Global Power Woman, NJBIZ Top 50 Women in Business, and Entrepreneur Leader of the Year.

Facebook: chayapamula
Instagram: chaya.pamula
LinkedIn: chayapamula
Profile: chaya.pamten.com

Christine Namusaazi
Founder, She Unit Uganda

Christine is a passionate advocate for women's empowerment and the founder of She Unit Uganda. She also serves as country director of Women of Africa Uganda and ambassador for SheChanges Climate. Since 2018, she has empowered over 400 women and girls through vocational training, financial literacy, and mentorship. Her work addresses period poverty, provides scholastic materials, and supports girls' education. Christine also raises climate awareness in schools and leads tree-planting initiatives. A champion of SDGs 5, 8, and 13, she believes that education, skills, and local innovation are key to uplifting marginalized communities and creating brighter futures for the next generation.

Facebook: She Unit Uganda
Instagram: sheunituganda
LinkedIn: Christine Namusaazi
sheunituganda.org

Clayton Platt
Founder/Principal, InnerEdge Consulting; Senior Facilitator and Program Consultant—Meditation4Leadership, Host—Magic in the Moment—Mindfulness in Real Time Podcast

Clayton is the founder of InnerEdge Consulting and a senior facilitator with Meditation4Leadership, where he helps professionals and organizations integrate mindfulness into leadership. With a background in financial services and high-level nonprofit fundraising, Clayton brings a unique, real-world perspective to cultivating presence, resilience, and authentic connection. He is the host of the *Mindfulness in Real Time* podcast, exploring how mindfulness can drive professional success and personal well-being through insightful conversations and practical strategies. Since March 2020, Clayton has led a weekly virtual Friday-morning mindfulness class, guiding participants to bridge theory and practice for lasting growth. His work empowers leaders to navigate challenges with clarity and intention, fostering meaningful impact in both their organizations and communities.

Facebook: Meditation4Leadership
Instagram: meditation4leadership
LinkedIn: Meditation4Leadership
YouTube: @meditation4leadership
X: Meditation4lead
Meditation4Leadership.org

Debra Rizzi
President & Partner, Rizco

Debra is the president and cofounder of Rizco, a brand-led marketing agency delivering strategic, design-driven solutions that make a measurable impact. With over thirty years of experience, she helps brands uncover what makes them matter through a people-first, purpose-driven approach. A graduate of Bucknell University, her career began in finance and evolved through creative leadership at global PR firm Porter Novelli, followed by more than two decades of entrepreneurship. Debra serves as co-president of the Wall Business and Finance Academy and sits on the New Jersey Chamber of Commerce Board of Directors. She has been honored by NJBIZ as one of the 50 Best Women in Business, Empowering Women, and 40 Under 40, and is an inductee into the Advertising Hall of Fame of New Jersey. A breast cancer survivor, youth advocate, and USA Gymnastics Level 10 Judge, Debra leads with authenticity, resilience, and a commitment to lasting impact.

Facebook: Rizco
Instagram: Debrarizzi
Instagram: Rizcodesign
LinkedIn: Debra Rizzi
LinkedIn: Rizco
Rizco.com

Deborah "Dee" Baker
Founder & CEO, Beyond the Uniform, LLC; US Air Force Veteran; CEO Women Operating in Overflow

Dee is a transformative leader, author, and advocate for women in service and leadership. A US Air Force veteran, she founded Beyond the Uniform (BTU) to help women step beyond roles and titles to lead with authenticity, courage, and purpose. She also established Women Operating in Overflow (WOO), a 501(c)(3) nonprofit dedicated to helping women heal, grow, and live with peace and power.

With more than thirty years in operations, leadership, and consulting, Dee has guided high-performing teams and multimillion-dollar programs. A two-time National Women of Color Award recipient, she was also honored with the Institute for Global Understanding Award from Monmouth University, recognizing her commitment to advancing peace, empathy, and cross-cultural understanding through leadership and service.

LinkedIn: Dee Baker
beyondtheuniforms.com

Deborah Koenigsberger
Founder & CEO Hearts of Gold Inc. & Owner, Noir et Blanc

Deborah is the founder of Hearts of Gold, a New York City nonprofit that has transformed the lives of more than 35,000 homeless mothers and children since 1994. Inspired by an encounter with a young mother and her three-year-old daughter sleeping in a cardboard box and by the song *Take the Time Out* by her idol Stevie Wonder, Deborah set out to break cycles of poverty and hopelessness. Before launching Hearts of Gold, she built a thriving career as a fashion model and stylist, and since 1989 has owned Noir et Blanc, her French-themed women's boutique in Manhattan. A graduate of NYU who speaks French, German, and Italian, Deborah is a devoted wife and mother of two, dedicated to reimagining futures—one family at a time.

Instagram: debkberger
Instagram: heartsofgoldnyc
heartsofgold.org

Fred C. Wasiak
Founder & Owner, Humanics Consulting
Creator: Outdoors With Papa

Fred is a people-centered, purpose-driven servant leader with more than 40 years of experience in human services and community development. His career spans impactful leadership roles — including 27 years with the YMCA, key positions at Goodwill Industries of Southern New Jersey and Philadelphia, and serving as President and CEO of the Food Bank of South Jersey.

In 2013, Fred founded Humanics Consulting, LLC, where he provides consulting, training, keynote speaking, and leadership development to nonprofit leaders and organizations.

Widely recognized for his servant leadership, Fred has earned numerous regional honors, including South Jersey Biz's Power 50, NPO Executive of the Year (2025), South Jersey Magazine's Men of the Year (2022), and South Jerseyan of the Year – Nonprofit Sector (2021). A lover of the outdoors, Fred lives in South Jersey with his wife, Betsy, and enjoys time with their growing family.

Web: humanicsconsulting.com
Instagram: humanicsconsulting
LinkedIn: Fred C. Wasiak
YouTube: @outdoorswithpapa

Helen Archontou, MSW, LSW
CEO, YWCA Northern New Jersey

Helen has served as CEO of YWCA Northern New Jersey for over 14 years, leading with a deep commitment to advancing gender equity and eliminating racism. Under her guidance, the organization has strengthened its mission and expanded its reach across five counties. She has centered the YW's racial justice work on empowering individuals to become catalysts for the systemic changes our communities urgently need.

Helen has also advanced innovative workforce development programs for women—particularly nonwhite women—creating pathways to meaningful careers and long-term financial independence. Her vision for empowering girls is reflected in the leadership workshops she helped develop, designed to remove barriers, and prepare future changemakers.

A core focus of her leadership is supporting survivors of sexual violence and trauma. She has expanded programs that ensure all individuals feel recognized, validated, and supported throughout their healing journeys.

Through her own ongoing practice of listening and learning, Helen has built strong partnerships that foster a more inclusive and empathetic community. As a visionary leader, she has embedded advocacy into every area of the YW's work, strengthening its ability to drive lasting change.

Facebook: YWCA Northern New Jersey
Facebook: Helen Archontou
Instagram: @ywcannj @helenarchontou
LinkedIn: Helen Archontou
LinkedIn: YWCA Northern New Jersey
ywcannj.org

Janet Kotsakis
Chief People Officer, Food Bank of South Jersey

As chief people officer at the Food Bank of South Jersey, Janet leads the development of HR systems while fostering a culture where staff can thrive. A lifelong learner, she is passionate about sharing professional development opportunities and ensuring every team member's talents are maximized. Before transitioning into HR, Janet built a successful career in corporate philanthropy and marketing, bringing a unique perspective to her nonprofit leadership. At the Food Bank, she collaborates across departments on internal communications, employee engagement, compliance, and events. Janet holds an MA in Professional Communication from LaSalle University, a BA from Arcadia University, and is SHRM-CP certified. She serves on the Feeding America HR Council and is an active member of the Tri-State HR Management Association.

Facebook: Food Bank of South Jersey
Instagram: foodbanksj
LinkedIn: Janet Kotsakis
LinkedIn: Food Bank of South Jersey
foodbanksj.org

JD Wilson
Founder, Lead U; Military Veteran

JD is a military veteran turned elementary school teacher who went on to found Lead U, an interactive education company using play to teach leadership, resilience, and kindness. Since 2016, Lead U has reached more than 1.2 million students worldwide, empowering young people to lead with authenticity and compassion. JD is also a children's book author, filmmaker, yoga instructor, and proud uncle. His work spans combat zones, classrooms, and crowded school assemblies, blending movement, mindfulness, and meaningful moments to inspire personal growth. Whether on stage or in small-group workshops, JD's mission is to create experiences that spark connection, build confidence, and equip individuals of all ages with the tools to navigate life with resilience, empathy, and a strong sense of purpose.

Facebook: Lead U
Instagram: lead_u_
LinkedIn: JD Wilson
leaduthere.com

Jennifer Devi Chauhan
Cofounder & Executive Director,
Project Write Now/Certified
Trauma-Informed Yoga Instructor

Jennifer is a writer, educator, and cofounder/executive director of Project Write Now, a nonprofit transforming lives through the power of writing. Since 2014, she has led its expansion into a trusted partner for nearly 100 schools and organizations, reaching more than 12,000 youth and adults with expressive and creative writing programs. In 2021, she launched PWN India, extending the mission globally. With more than thirty years in education— as a journalist, high school English and Creative Writing teacher, and nonprofit leader—Jennifer creates inclusive, trauma-informed spaces where all voices can be heard. Honored by Monmouth Arts for her impact on the arts community, she holds degrees from Teachers College, Columbia University, and Villanova University, and is currently writing a memoir on grief, loss, and reinvention.

Facebook: Project Write Now
Instagram: jenchauhan
Instagram: projectwritenow
LinkedIn: Jennifer Chauhan
LinedIn: Project Write Now
projectwritenow.org

Katie Marra

Undergraduate Student in Entomology and Ecology, Rutgers University

Katie is a student at Rutgers University pursuing a double major in entomology and ecology, with a focus on the conservation of pollinators. Conducting research in Rutgers' entomology lab, she studies native bees in urban environments, with recent NYC-based work earning her the President's Award for Research from the Entomological Society of America. Passionate about connecting people to the natural world, Katie leads educational workshops in New York City community gardens, inspiring others to protect pollinators and the ecosystems they sustain. She is committed to bridging the gap between the needs of a growing population and a sustainable environment, seeing each research endeavor and community engagement as a step toward a healthier, more harmonious relationship with the planet we share.

LinkedIn: Katie Marra
Instagram: katie_marra

Lenny Dave
Comedy Historian, Humor Camp Cofounder, Speaker, Author, Humorist

Lenny is a nationally recognized comedy historian, speaker, author, and humorist whose creative mission is simple: To make a positive difference in people's lives and help bring an end to "toxic sameness." For over thirty-five years, he has informed and entertained audiences with nostalgic, interactive programs celebrating the funny people who have made us laugh for decades. As the first and only speaker to perform in both the Red Skelton Entertainment Series and the Oliver Hardy Festival, Lenny honors the legacies of so many of our favorite comedy icons while inspiring the audience to find joy in the present. Cofounder of Humor Camp, he also served as international president of the Association for Applied & Therapeutic Humor and sits on the Advisory Board of the Borscht Belt Museum. Fun fact: Lenny's caught fourteen foul balls at Major League Baseball games!

Facebook: Lenny Dave
LinkedIn: Lenny Dave
lennydave.com

Lisa Clark

International Amateur Race Car Driver, Ferrari Challenge Series, and Endurance Racing

Growing up with her father, a man deeply passionate about cars, Lisa absorbed that same love for engines and speed, even if she didn't realize it at the time. Years later, after marriage and building several businesses together, she found herself drawn back to that early passion. What began as a hobby evolved into something far more—a defining part of who she is. Today, racing is more than a pastime; it's a reflection of her drive and spirit. Lisa is now on a journey of self-discovery, fueled by her love for the sport and strengthened by the lessons and determination she's gained along the way.

Facebook: Lisa Clark
Instagram: racer.mom

Mohan Metla

Founder & Owner, Mohan Group LLC

Mohan is a global marketing, technology, and strategy executive with over fifteen years of experience driving digital transformation, CRM strategy, and data-driven growth across B2C and B2B sectors. As founder and principal of Mohan Group LLC, he leads marketing innovation, customer experience, and real estate projects in domestic and international markets. Known for his expertise in predictive analytics and cross-platform strategy, Mohan partners with C-suite leaders to deliver scalable business solutions. He recently completed the MIT Professional Education – Applied Data Science Program, enhancing his skills in AI and advanced analytics for executive decision-making. A champion of inclusive leadership and talent development, Mohan has built and led diverse global teams, aligning strategy, analytics, and customer engagement to accelerate sustainable organizational growth.

LinkedIn: www.linkedin.com/in/mmetla2022
mohangroupllc.com

Nicholas Marco

Entrepreneur; Partner, Marco Region Enterprises; Owner, Hand & Stone Massage, Drybar, Sweat 440; Founder, Free Cash Flow Advisor

Nicholas has been part of the *Hand & Stone Massage and Facial Spa* story since before its first location opened in 2004—a brand he named at just fourteen. Today, he is one of the company's largest franchisees with eleven New Jersey locations and serves as regional developer of Ohio, overseeing twenty locations with a goal of thirty-five. Expanding his portfolio, Nicholas is also a franchisee of *Drybar* and *Sweat440*. In 2023, his businesses generated nearly $28 million in revenue.

Leading an organization of more than 500 employees, Nicholas is passionate about team building, leadership development, and empowering franchisees and managers. His background as an ICU Registered Nurse deepened his dedication to health and wellness. Committed to helping others realize their potential, he shares insights twice a month on his podcast, *The Opportunity Coach*.

LinkedIn: Nicholas Marco
Instagram: nicholasmarco_ceo

Nicol Nicola, DBA

Director of Economic & Demographic Research, NJDOL; Adjunct Professor; Leadership Training Facilitator

Nicol leads a dynamic team focused on analyzing and communicating labor market and demographic trends. A sought-after speaker and advisor, Dr. Nicola travels across the country to share strategies for using data to drive evidence-based decision-making. She also mentors and coaches executives, helping them uncover their leadership style and develop a personal leadership philosophy.

LinkedIn: Nicol Nicola

Sarah Jakle, MSW, MPP
Founder & Executive Director,
DemocraShe

Sarah is the founder and executive director of DemocraShe, a nonpartisan national nonprofit dedicated to empowering historically underserved high school girls to see themselves as leaders, voters, civically engaged citizens, and future elected officials. Her career includes serving as Get Out the Vote Director for the California National Organization for Women and National Outreach Director for Field Team 6, where she championed women's political participation and innovative voter registration. Blending civic leadership training with brain science, Sarah equips young women to break barriers, lead with confidence, and claim running for office as their birthright. A graduate of Yale (Phi Beta Kappa) with an MSW from USC and a MPP from UCLA, she is a former Obama Organizing for Action Fellow.

Facebook: DemocraShe
Instagram: democrasheorg
LinkedIn: Sarah Jakle
democrashe.org

Steven M. Cohen
Author of *Leading from Within*;
Cofounder & Chair,
Meditation4Leadership

Steven is the author of *Leading from Within: A Guide to Maximizing Your Effectiveness Through Meditation*, the cofounder and chair of the board of Meditation4Leadership, which brings the benefits of mindfulness and meditation practices to the workplace. He is a partner in an AmLaw 50 law firm and a frequent speaker on the personal and professional benefits of mindfulness and meditation practice.

Facebook: Meditation4Leadership
Instagram: meditation4leadership
LinkedIn: Meditation4Leadership
YouTube: @meditation4leadership
X: Meditation4lead
meditation4leadership.org

Tanya Newbould

Life Transformation Strategist; ACC/ICF Certified Coach; Speaker, Entrepreneur, Author, Producer, Actress; Founder, DelPozzo Jewelry & SOZO Heart

Tanya is a Life Transformation Strategist, number one bestselling author, executive coach, entrepreneur, and creative visionary dedicated to helping others rise, heal, and thrive. After two decades as an actress and producer, she founded five businesses, including Del Pozzo Jewelry and SOZO Heart, a wellness brand inspired by medicinal-grade essential oils. A certified ACC coach through the International Coaching Federation and Licensed Academy Trainer, Tanya guides individuals and organizations through profound shifts in mindset and performance. A fierce advocate for maternal mental health, she co-created and co-produced the acclaimed documentary *When the Bough Breaks*, now seen in over sixty countries. Her mission is to help others awaken to their worth, ignite their purpose, and step boldly into the life they were meant to live.

Instagram: tanyanewbould
Instagram: sozoheart
Instagram: delpozzojewelry
tanyanewbould.com
sozoheart.org
Delpozzojewelry.luxury

Tara Coffman
Financial Industry Professional

Tara is a wife, mother, friend, and 100 percent Jersey Girl. She grew up in Woodbridge, NJ, attended Douglass College, and for the last seventeen years has lived in Jackson, NJ, raising her kids and taking care of her family. Tara has worked everything from the midnight shift at Quick Chek to store manager at Walgreens, and everything in between. With an emphasis on honesty and integrity and a desire to make a difference in the lives of others, she has created a deeply satisfying financial practice where she empowers others to make informed decisions regarding their financial lives. Tara has changed and reinvented herself many times over the years, and she is sure she will do it many times more. In fact, the only thing certain in life is change!

Facebook: Tara Coffman
Instagram: tlc0506
LinkedIn: Tara Coffman

Tara Marie Stemkovsky
Creator & Host, *True Crime Matters with Tara Marie*

Tara is a storyteller and advocate whose work is rooted in resilience, creativity, and purpose. With a background in broadcast journalism and film theory from Rutgers University, she is committed to amplifying nuanced, empathetic narratives for those often silenced or overlooked. As creator and host of *True Crime Matters with Tara Marie*, she examines true crime through a trauma-informed lens, shaped by her own experience when her family was thrust into the national spotlight after her father's arrest. Her work holds space for victims while exploring the broader contexts—such as addiction, mental illness, and cycles of abuse—that can influence behavior. Reaching millions, Tara's storytelling has fueled real-world advocacy, including renewed attention to a high-profile case now under review by the LA Innocence Project.

Facebook: True Crime Matters
Instagram: truecrimematters
Patreon: TrueCrimeMatters
X: TrueCrimewithTM
TikTok: truecrimematter
YouTube: True Crime Matters with Tara Marie

Terese Rölke

Starting a New Chapter in My Life

Born and raised in Brooklyn, NY, Terese is a passionate community leader, storyteller, and lifelong advocate for kindness and service. With a degree in TV/Radio from Brooklyn College, she began her career at American Express, where she produced impactful corporate video content and launched a successful internship program. Her dedication to mentoring and uplifting others led her to create meaningful initiatives like Take Our Daughters to Work Day experiences and community events promoting unity.

After marrying and moving to Monmouth County, NJ, she deepened her commitment to service—volunteering as a Cub Scout Leader, PTO president, and Life Vest Inside ambassador and group leader. She led the local Worldwide Dance for Kindness for seven years, bringing joy and connection to hundreds. While serving as executive director of the Monmouth Regional Chamber of Commerce until 2026, Terese continues to champion collaboration, growth, and kindness.

LinkedIn: Terese Rolke

Tisha Janigian
President & Founder, SHE IS HOPE LA,
Broker & Owner - SHE IS HOPE Realty

Tisha is the president and founder of SHE IS HOPE LA, a nonprofit dedicated to educating and empowering single mothers. Inspired by her own journey after divorce in 2012—when she faced life with no money, credit, or assets—Tisha built SHE IS HOPE LA to provide the tools she once needed herself, offering a "hand up" rather than a handout. She is also the owner and broker of SHE IS HOPE Realty, a full-service California brokerage handling residential, commercial, luxury, and investment transactions, with a percentage of all commissions supporting the nonprofit. Through her leadership, Tisha transforms challenge into opportunity, modeling hard work and resilience for her two sons and showing that with determination, adversity can lead to purpose and the fulfillment of dreams.

Facebook: Tisha Janigian, SHE IS HOPE LA, SHE IS HOPE Realty
Instagram: sheishopela and sheishoperealty
LinkedIn: Tisha Janigian
LinkedIn: SHE IS HOPE LA
sheishoperealty.com

TODAY IS THE DAY CHANGEMAKERS PODCAST UNITES THE WORLD!

The Today is the Day Changemakers Podcast has been downloaded across the globe, including:

Afghanistan
Albania
Anguilla
Argentina
Australia
Austria
Azerbaijan
Bangladesh
Barbados
Belgium
Belize
Benin
Bolivia
Bosnia and Herzegovina
Botswana
Brazil
Bulgaria
Burkina Faso
Canada
Cayman Islands
Chile
China
Colombia
The Democratic Republic of the Congo
Costa Rica
Croatia
Curaçao

Cyprus
Czechia
Denmark
Djibouti
Dominica
Estonia
Ethiopia
Finland
France
French Polynesia
Georgia
Germany
Ghana
Greece
Grenada
Guadeloupe
Guatemala
Guinea
Hong Kong
Hungary
Iceland
India
Indonesia
Iran
Iraq
Ireland
Israel
Italy
Jamaica

Japan
Jordan
Kazakhstan
Kenya
Kosovo
Lao People's Democratic Republic
Lebanon
Lithuania
Luxembourg
Madagascar
Malaysia
Mali
Malta
Mauritania
Mauritius
Mexico
Moldova
Nepal
Netherlands
New Caledonia
New Zealand
Nicaragua
Niger
Nigeria
North Macedonia
Norway
Pakistan

State of Palestine
Panama
Papua New Guinea
Paraguay
Peru
Philippines
Poland
Portugal
Puerto Rico
Réunion
Romania
Russian Federation
Rwanda
Saint Lucia
Saint Vincent and the Grenadines
Samoa
Saudi Arabia
Serbia
Seychelles
Sierra Leone
Singapore
Slovakia
Slovenia
Somalia
South Africa
South Korea

South Sudan
Spain
Sweden
Switzerland
Syrian Arab Republic
Türkiye
Taiwan
Tajikistan
Tanzania
Thailand
Trinidad and Tobago
Turkey
Turks and Caicos Islands
Uganda
Ukraine
United Arab Emirates
United Kingdom
United States
Uruguay
Venezuela
Vietnam
Yemen
Zambia
Zimbabwe

We asked the guests from the very first season of the
Today is the Day Changemakers Podcast to share one word
that best describes them as a changemaker. Their words, energy,
and impact became the foundation for what you see below.

WE ARE **TODAY IS THE DAY** CHANGEMAKERS

Sharing our vulnerability, **resilience**, inspiration, persistence,
enthusiasm, optimism, influence, authenticity, compassion,
strategy, perseverance, **patience**, and passion.

We are agile, **solvers**, adaptive, openminded, **motivated**,
lifelong learners that expand our bigness through storytelling.

As Impactpreneurs **we are influencers** and strategists.

We believe that everyone can **achieve their goals** because the possibilities
of what we can do as one global community sharing ideas is **endless.**

Together,

we are champions of hope.

What word(s) describe you as a **changemaker?**

TODAY is the DAY

you cannot go back to YESTERDAY,
and you do not yet own TOMORROW.

TodayIsTheDayLiveIt.com

Scan to Stay Connected!

https://todayisthedayliveit.com